HOW MONEY TALKS

Other titles in the UKCP Series:

HOW MONEY TALKS

Lesley Murdin

On behalf of the United Kingdom Council
for Psychotherapy

KARNAC

The author and publisher are grateful to the following for permission to quote the following material:

Madsen Gubi, P. (2010). *A Qualitative Exploration of the Similarities and Differences between Counselling and Spiritual Accompaniment* (pp. 8, 45, 54). Unpublished dissertation, Anglia Ruskin University.

First published in 2012 by
Karnac Books Ltd
118 Finchley Road
London NW3 5HT

British Library Cataloguing in Publication Data

A C.I.P. for this book is available from the British Library

ISBN-13: 978-1-78049-067-0

Typeset by V Publishing Solutions Pvt Ltd., Chennai, India

Printed in Great Britain

www.karnacbooks.com

This book is dedicated to my patients and supervisees, who have taught me much of what I know

CONTENTS

ACKNOWLEDGEMENTS

I would like to thank the editors at Karnac Books, especially Heward Wilkinson for his wisdom, scholarship, and willingness to encourage and help me in researching and structuring the book.

My thanks are always due to Meg Errington for all that she contributes to my development as a psychotherapist and in the past to my own psychotherapist and supervisors. I would like to thank my husband Paul Murdin for his generous practical help and encouragement.

My love of English literature is responsible for some of the illustrations and for my background and understanding of people. For this I owe much to my teachers, chiefly Kathleen Donnelly and Dorothy Bednarowska.

The description of the case of Alice is fictional and should not be taken as representing any actual person living or dead. Her story, and the people and organisations in it, are also fictitious. As in all novels and in case studies in books about psychotherapy, the study is based on a variety of my experiences and understanding as the author of the book, but it does not relate to any actual people or events.

ABOUT THE AUTHOR

Lesley Murdin practises as a psychoanalytic psychotherapist. She teaches and supervises in many contexts and has considerable experience in running psychotherapy organisations. She has worked for the registering bodies UKCP and BPC, chairing committees over many years. She was CEO and National Director of WPF Therapy and is now Chair of the psychoanalytic section of the Foundation for Psychotherapy and Counselling. She has published numerous books and papers.

INTRODUCTION

The idea for this book came to me because of the emphasis on money that prevails in the consumer society in which we live, especially since the global financial recession of 2008. As a result of general uncertainty, people from many shades of political opinion focussed thought and emotions on wealth, wealth creation, and how people achieve and retain their personal wealth. An unprecedented level of media and individual attention has focussed on the morality or otherwise of the means of acquiring wealth. In the UK, two groups have received public scorn and anger. Politicians were tried and convicted for claiming undeserved and in some cases illegal levels of payments for expenses. This was ascribed to greed. The second group consisted of bankers, who irresponsibly sold mortgages and other "products" that could not be sustained by the people concerned from their income. The bankers too have been accused of greed in seeking to maximise their profits without paying attention to the effect on their customers. Both of these groups have caused much pain and distress. The bankers in particular have been accused of causing global financial difficulties. Whether or not this is a fair representation of where the responsibility lies, it has given rise to subsequent arguments about who is responsible for too much borrowing: is it the borrower or the lender? The doubt about this certainly reinforces Polonius' dictum that we should be neither a borrower nor a lender (Hamlet, Act I, Scene iii).

Questions about the morality of borrowing and lending take us back to the whole basis of modern consumer societies. What underwrites or underpins the money that we use to buy and sell? We no longer expect national banks to hold gold to the value of the currency circulating, although it is noticeable that in times of trouble people rush to buy gold as it is seen as a safe haven. The whole concept of a "safe haven" implies that money makes us feel safe and without it we feel helpless and impotent. We must also put it in a safe place so that we can keep it and find it. This led to my interest in the developmental implications of the individual's relationship to money: in what sense does it take over from the primary relationship with the breast or early feeding? There has been thinking about the historical development of money and its meaning and use in each culture but I have not found much attention being paid to the development in each individual of the attitude to money that is apparent in the adult.

The book will therefore attempt to look at these general themes using examples taken from novels and from clinical experience. The main illustration is the case history of Alice which is told in Part I. As is required by the codes of ethics of psychotherapists, this is a fictional case history, but it does draw on actual experience, mine and other people's. The case of Alice is written in detail, developing her story and the story of her relationship with getting and spending and with what else matters to her. The subsequent chapters then look at the aspects of the symbolism, use and management of money with Alice's experience as an illustration.

The clinical importance of money is hard to exaggerate. It is an essential part of the therapeutic process. It has to be discussed at the outset of therapy, and then at periodic intervals subsequently as invoices are given out and money handed over. Some therapists[1] charge a fee in each session, so every individual session will bring up the management of money. For all therapists, payment is a revelation, showing the way in which the patient relates to money as reality and as a symbol.

The patient also reveals his values and the hierarchy in which people are valued at one level and property and goods at another. The patient has an economy in which there is a rate of exchange. One of the purposes of this book is to consider the process of exchange and how it interacts with valuing. Since money is by its nature a symbol and its referent is constantly changing, the therapist can derive a significant and useful amount of information from the patient's treatment of money in the consulting room. She can also see how her own pathology interacts with that of her patient to produce the unique quality of each relationship.

In Part II the main areas that are considered are the history and symbolism of money, the management of money and its implications for the individual. Chapter Seven deals with the ways in which we use money to reveal the pain and suffering of which human beings are capable. Money is related closely to control, omnipotence, and the ability to hold on or to let go. For these reasons it plays a part in many mental states that are generally grouped under the heading of obsessional traits. Chapter Eight takes the questions about how these states of mind develop and considers the developmental processes for an individual. Chapter Nine considers the individual in a social context where money operates at all levels to link and separate us. The last chapter of this section, Chapter Ten, considers social questions about the funding of psychological treatment as a question of national and also personal importance.

Part III deals with money from the therapist's point of view. The two chapters, Chapters Eleven and Twelve, focus on the consulting room and the way in which the themes of payments, gifts and debts are played out in each person's therapy. How each therapist obtains the considerable amount of money needed for her own training is also formative on her attitudes to money, and the way in which her background affects her behaviour.

My own theoretical background is psychoanalytic and I write from this point of view, although other modalities are taken into account. "Psychoanalytic" implies basic assumptions on the existence and accessibility of the dynamic unconscious. It includes the relevance of patterns of symbolism and meaning reflected in patterns of behaviour that can be understood and changed. The relationship in the consulting room makes it a place where all kinds of pain and suffering will be revealed both to the sufferer and the therapist so that there can be hope of changing them.

The writer has an integrated analytic training in which the ideas of Freud, Klein and Jung were all respected and would be used to suit each individual patient. The modern French school was mainly represented by Jacques Lacan.

Note

1. The term therapist is used for psychoanalyst, counsellor, and psychotherapist unless one of these is explicit. The male pronoun is used for the patient and the female for the therapist to represent the predominance of women in the profession and avoid the clumsiness of the plural pronoun.

PART I

MONEY TALKS

I'm a mess

A lice got off the bus and thought "This is it. This is what I have decided to do and it must be all right." She looked at her watch, anxious to be on time but not sure exactly where the house was. She thought she would need about five minutes to walk from the bus stop. She really wanted to get there on time because her friend Rosalie who was already seeing a psychotherapist had told her that that they are very hot on times so that you have to arrive dead on time and you will be asked to leave after exactly fifty minutes. Alice wanted to look like someone who knew how things were done.

The bus had dropped her in a busy main road with narrow footpaths and 1950s houses, beginning to look a little seedy although they all had gardens. She noticed that the busy road didn't stop people from having at least one car each with the result that about half the gardens had been transformed into hard standing. "Hard standing," she thought. "Yes, standing is hard. I wonder whether she will expect me to lie down."

The map of the area was in Alice's mind, although she had forgotten to bring the map page that she had printed and then left on the printer. She often did that. Maybe the therapist would say whether she was getting early-onset Alzheimer's, whatever that was. She crossed the road and walked along two blocks, looking for the address that she had been given. It was a bit further than she had expected but she hadn't really begun to panic when she found the road with the right name. She hoped that the house numbers would be clear because she was a bit short sighted and she worried about having to go up to people's front doors to see who they were. Well, not who they were but what their number was. Some people obviously think it matters to identify themselves with lovely big, clear numbers that you can easily see and others don't care whether you can see them or not. The road wound on down a hill, now with trees, making it into an avenue. "This is better," she thought, although the houses were still semi-detached and all still identical. She found two numbers so that she could count her way to the right house. She walked more and more slowly but got there just the same.

In the driveway was a big, dusty Volvo estate car. Alice squeezed past it to the front door wondering whether she was being watched from the window. It was two minutes to the hour, so she thought that was good enough. A small woman with grey hair in an untidy short cut answered the bell quickly. "She *was* watching me," thought Alice. There wasn't much time to think more about that, as the woman smiled warmly and said, "You must be Alice, come in. I'm Margaret." That worried Alice. Rosalie had told her that formality was important to psychoanalytic psychotherapists. She ought to be calling herself "Dr Andrews."

Alice followed down a passage right to the back of the house, past several firmly closed doors. She wondered who might be in these rooms and whether one of the doors might open. That led to the question of whether Margaret might have a family. She looked about fifty so probably no young children but you never know. Was she married? Alice wondered about that briefly and thought she would ask her. She was shown into a small room with two chairs and a divan. Margaret gestured towards the further chair. That was a relief. She was not expected to lie down. Besides, other people had been lying there. It might even still be warm. For the moment Alice was glad that someone else was taking charge. Margaret sat down in the other chair and smiled. "What brings you here?" she asked. Alice gave another sigh of relief. She had thought she would sit there in silence while Margaret waited for her to say something. At least she seemed to want to hear what Alice had to say.

"I am in a mess," Alice said and explained.

> I am losing everything. My husband has been diagnosed with prostate cancer. I had a really good job and I am losing it. That's not all of course but I'll tell you about the job first. I have run a small charity here in Bradford called Mental Freedom and I made a mistake and the mistake that I made came back to haunt me. I'll tell you about how it started. I suppose it goes back to the days when I had my children and come to think of it, maybe that also has its roots in my own childhood. Well of course it must. How could my mistakes as a parent not have some connection with the mistakes as well as the good things that I experienced with my own parents?
>
> I have an Oxbridge degree and I felt that I ought to have an interesting career. Because I married a distinguished scientist, my career to some extent had to follow along behind him. That makes me feel terrible now because …

Alice stopped because she did not want to cry but she could feel that she was going to. Margaret said nothing; she sat quite still and gave just the slightest nod which clearly said that she was listening and waiting to hear what Alice wanted to say.

Alice turned her head to look out of the window and focussed on what she could see of the small garden. She likes flowers, Alice thought. But how can she let it be so wild. The lawn appeared to have been cut but round the edges there were wild profusions of weeds and flowers. Nothing seemed to have been excluded. It made her think of her garden at home. "I like your garden," she said, "even though it reminds me of mine."

> Our garden has become a scene for argument and in a way it sums up how we have wasted opportunities with each other. I can see Oliver, standing in the kitchen doorway. I was outside trying to weed the bed which I might use to plant vegetables one day. At the moment, the best I hope for is to keep the weeds at bay enough that it doesn't return completely to its natural, unregenerate state. I can impose my will on it a little. Besides I like the totally undemanding feeling of kneeling there on the ground with nothing more worrying to decide than whether this green stem belongs to a weed or a potential flower.

Perhaps I had a romantic delusion that I can be like Mary in *The Secret Garden* and that Oliver would come out and join me like the poor crippled Colin and be calmed by the regenerative power of the garden. A robin often comes and sits nearby watching me, his black beady eye measuring just how much I am turning over the soil. "Well, all right" I tell him, "I'm not the world's most expert gardener but I am doing my best." He shakes his head just a little: "Not good enough I'm afraid." Then I turn to Oliver who does tell me what he is thinking: "What on earth are you doing? You need to work systematically from one end to the other. Don't just dot about like that taking things out wherever you feel like it."

"Come and help me then if you know so much about it."

"You know perfectly well that I haven't the time. I have to finish an article for the publishers by the end of the week."

Before I had time to list any of the things that I also had to do by the end of the week, he had turned and retreated into the darkness of his study. That sort of exchange took its toll. I would feel furious and storm around making dinner in a way which was to be read as a complex message of protest and injured martyrdom. That was the way it usually went. Then came the never-to–be-forgotten day.

He was leaning against the door jamb of the kitchen door as usual, but instead of commenting on my gardening ineptitude, he just said "Come into the study later; I need to talk to you." I was surprised but noting the tone of his voice, which had a quality in it that I couldn't quite place, I realised that this was not the usual combative situation. Something else was going on. I pulled out a few more random weeds in a desultory, disorganised way, feeling very guilty that I still had not been organised about working from one end to the other. Oliver was right really. It would be much better to use my energy in a focussed way. Maybe I did the same at work. Perhaps that was what was going wrong there. I sat back on my heels wiping hair out of my face with a muddy glove. The robin flew off in disgust. If I wasn't going to work, and expose grubs and beetles, he wasn't going to wait around.

My mind started to process my anxiety about Oliver. Was he going to tell me that he had found someone better and would leave me? Had he found someone really organised who would at least pay attention to what he said? I knew I was stubborn and determined. One of the Trustees had said in a meeting in front of all the others: "Don't worry about her. She's as tough as old boots." I thought at the time he just wanted to pave the way for making more demands on me to produce even more money out of nowhere, but I have thought about it often since and I realise now that perhaps I am stronger than I had realised before. How much strength would I need?

I ran over in my mind a whole set of terrible scenarios. Oliver was working in the university as a lecturer in biological science where, although he didn't make a great deal of money, his job was secure enough. I could not imagine that there was a serious problem with his job. So that left him. And me. They say that your whole life runs before you when you are drowning. I think I had a partial version of one of those moments just then.

I thought about my job. I had been unhappier than I had ever been before, just when I should have been most content. I had managed to achieve a high status job. I was appointed Chief Executive of Mental Freedom doing work that I passionately supported. What we did was support prisoners by training and managing a team of counsellors who would go in to support the staff in the prisons across Yorkshire and Lancashire. We also worked with probation officers and provided counsellors who would work with ex-offenders. The work was difficult and demanding and we had to be very careful of our mostly young staff. I had enjoyed the role that I had in the training initially, after teaching in various schools. I realised that teaching adults was still challenging but in a totally different way from teaching adolescents in schools. When I was teaching children, I had needed presence. Presence I didn't have, or at least not enough of the right sort. I was short and quietly spoken and neither of those are good qualities in a class of 35 noisy adolescents. The challenge with our adult counselling students was mostly about the actual knowledge and theory that I was presenting. They needed to know about the prison population and about the techniques that had been found to help them. I could cope with that. In fact I enjoyed it.

I was now regretting that my drive to be promoted that had led me to agree to apply for the post of Chief Executive when our much-respected boss left. As a charity all our doings are subject to the authority of the Board of Trustees. The BOT, as we called them, was chaired at the time by a retired banker who had a very good sense of both the need for the work that we do and how to keep a charity's head above water by making good friends and useful contacts in the world of business. I respected him and I think he liked me. In the interview he was generous to me and he must have given me the benefit of any doubt because there were some very serious candidates as I later discovered. One was a Vicar and a wonderful talker. Another was a colleague, Mike, whom I had known when he was on our staff. He had left and gone to work for another charity but he wanted now to come back and I knew that he was a most accomplished talker.

As an internal candidate, I knew that I had advantages and disadvantages. The Trustees knew my record and at that stage I was proud of it. I had good feedback from all my teaching groups and even though there was sometimes an odd one who would find my style irritating or my attitude to minority groups not gung-ho enough, mostly they seemed to find me open and encouraging as I wanted to be. They appreciated the encouraging part and I loved doing the encouraging. I suppose I appropriated their achievements so that they became partly my achievements. Probably all teachers are doing that if they are honest. Is that fair? I am not sure.

Margaret shifted on her chair slightly but said nothing. Alice decided to go on:

On the other hand there were disadvantages to being on the inside. They knew that I had my limitations. I had only just learned to read accounts and had never had occasion to use Excel spread sheets so my knowledge was limited to setting up a sum but I certainly could not do anything much more complex than that. Other candidates could say "yes, yes, yes" when asked what they could do. Unless they were tested, no-one would know how true it was. We weren't tested. But they gave me the job anyway and my troubles began.

I thought I was invincible at that moment. I had the approval of the whole BOT in the sense that they all had to agree on my appointment. Marcus, the Chairman, told me that the whole group was delighted with my appointment but I later found out that he was being a little economical with the truth. At that stage though, I thought everything was fine. What I need to say now is what happened next. That is difficult because I don't even want to think about it myself, let alone tell anyone else.

I have to accept that to some extent I brought it on myself. The charity was not bringing in enough money. That was always the bottom line. We had supporters who donated small amounts, often a one-off small cheque when they felt they could manage to peel off a layer of their financial security and give it away. Most of them are over sixty five and are terrified that they will not have enough to get by when they are really old. Some of them have set up small direct debits. That's better but it doesn't bring in enough to keep us going. So what could I do? I did the only thing that seemed possible: I appointed a fund raiser. She was a delightful woman, with excellent credentials. She told us that she had a young baby but I was very careful not to discriminate against anyone for such reasons and I resolutely put it on one side and offered her the job based on her experience for other large and successful charities. That turned out to be the problem. Lana came in for her first morning about thirty minutes late. "So sorry," she breezed, "child care not yet properly in place. Be fine tomorrow." I didn't say anything but my heart sank. I took her to the desk that we had organised for her in a small but well equipped office. "It is a bit small," she said disapprovingly. "I don't know whether there'll be room for all my files. I will have a lot of files. Where are the current donor files?"

"Well," I said, "all the supporters are supposed to be on line but that is something we need you to check. Are you happy with the software? We did mention it at the interview."

"Yes, but I am a bit rusty. We'll take a look and see what I can do. I'll just sort out my things and maybe we can have a talk after that"

I was so taken aback at the general breeziness that I merely said "Yes. Fine. I'll expect you in my room at 10 o'clock."

"It would be much more useful if you were to come back here. Then we can sort out what the software will or will not do. That will be much quicker." I was starting to find this approach irritating: "There is more to consider than the donor data-base but I will come and make sure that you can use its full potential."

This conversation and the outcome in which I did exactly what Lana wanted me to and didn't complain about her lateness set the tone for the relationship that we had for the next six months. I somehow had the impression that she might just walk out if we didn't measure up to the standards of National Chest Foundation which she had worked for most recently. I needed results fast and I needed a successful fund raiser to save us from imminent disaster. Thinking she might leave was ridiculous and I don't know what made me worry about it. My problem turned out to be very different. That very first morning I just introduced Lana to several key staff. I took her to meet the receptionists first and then the administrators of the training group. They were all happy to know that our financial problems would soon be at an end and, they hoped, their salaries would be increased. I have to admit that none of us was earning very much. I was keen that the differential between my salary and the senior staff salaries should not be too great and had kept it at a relatively small number. We couldn't afford any more but I had said that increasing staff salaries was a high priority.

June Halliday, the manager of all the office staff took to Lana straight away. June had no children but she was very keen to have a baby soon and she got into a deep conversation with Lana at the first coffee break.

At lunchtime Lana knocked on my half open door "Come in," I said without enthusiasm. Lana breezed in.

"I've enjoyed meeting some of the staff this morning but now I would like to meet my administrator." I looked at her in surprise. "We told you that we are a small charity with very few staff. I can give you a few hours a week of help when you need something like envelopes stuffing or leaflets printing."

"You expect me to raise substantial amounts of money with no help!"

"No," I said shortly, "with a few hours a week."

"That will make it really difficult."

I thought we had better get down to what we expected from her rather than following this golden thread of what she expected us to do for her.

I soon discovered that the fund-raising that she had done for NCF could not be replicated for us. "First," she said, "I need to review your high worth donors."

"What," I asked "is a high worth donor? We just have donors."

"Oh come on. You must have some old dears who can fork out for you. I need to know how many you have so that we can sort out an event that will appeal to them."

"Yes," I agreed, "we want an event straight away. I believe that you made a lot of money from events when you were at NCF."

"You can't have an event straight away. You have to plan at least a year ahead and that's after I find out who we can invite."

"I thought you would know who to invite. Or find them."

"That's not my job. I will schmooze them for you but this is not health or children or donkeys, is it? Your donors will be very different from mine at NCF."

By this time I was extremely depressed. Like all charities, we needed a considerable sum each year from fund raising if we were to make ends meet. I knew that if we didn't find this money, we would not have enough reserves to meet the salary bill in six months' time at the end of the financial year. I had told the Trustees at the last BOT meeting I accepted the best hope was to appoint a really good fund raiser. They agreed, although one or two were sceptical. Our business man, Richard, who had run a firm of accountants, was totally enthusiastic. Lana had applied for the job and then withdrawn her application for a personal reason. When I told Richard about this he rang her up and the next thing I knew she was back on side. I don't know what he said to her but whatever it was, it worked. I was glad to get it settled but still doubtful about taking on someone who had to be persuaded to take on the job. Especially, I thought, we need someone who will enthusiastically support the work that we do and will persuade others to support it too. In addition she had asked the Trustees to pay her a salary that was £5,000 higher than we had offered. They immediately agreed.

Now that she had actually arrived, I thought, look what he's done. Richard had made it clear to me that I had been weak in accepting her decision to withdraw. So at the next BOT meeting he gave his report to the others saying how he had persuaded her that she would enjoy the work and they were full of praise for his charm and persuasive powers. I sat and said nothing as so often. They didn't seek to understand what I thought about it and I didn't volunteer to tell them.

Over the next six months, things followed a downward trajectory. It turned out as I had suspected that our donors were not of high worth but were all giving amounts like £25 per month. Lana was filled with righteous indignation: "Mean old bag. Why don't you ring her up and get her to double it. I bet she has stacks of money stored away."

"I really expected that *you* would be ringing people up and persuading them to give us more money."

"There is no point in me ringing them up. You know who they all are and you can talk to them much better than I can."

That sort of comment left me speechless with inhibited anger. She gradually went through the entire list of the elements of her job description, pointing out that I could actually do it much better than she could. I tried various approaches. At first I tried practical responses: I haven't the time and I want you to get to know the donors. She would decline to answer but would simply not do anything. I would go into her office and look at her screen. There might be a page of the data base but she was usually writing away in longhand in a scruffy notebook. The third or fourth time this happened I asked her what she was doing. She looked up, obviously irritated to be interrupted. "I am writing my journal" she said in a patient tone. I hesitated. It could be legitimate if she meant she was keeping a record of the work she was doing. "Why don't you keep it on line? There is a space for notes on each page of the database and you could order them by dates."

"This is too personal for that."

"If it's personal, is it appropriate to be doing it in working hours?"

"Of course it is. It helps me to work." I assimilated this for a few moments.

"Did I tell you about my cats?" she continued. "I have three cats and I love them to bits. The trouble is the Health Visitor says they present a danger to Justin. Apparently cats sit on top of babies and suffocate them. This may have happened in the course of human history but it doesn't mean that my cats would do it. The big male is called Tarzan but he's as gentle as a, as a … well he's not very gentle with birds of course but a baby isn't a bird. Why would he harm a baby? I'm just keeping a record of how he is behaving every morning so that I can tell that bitch where she gets off. And I couldn't come to work if I had to stay at home instead of the baby sitter, so you see I must keep this journal up to date."

"How are you getting on with the idea of a big event?" I ventured.

"Haven't had time to think about it. I have to do all the data entry myself because the admin help you are giving me is useless."

"Well, let's start to think about it now. How about a dinner with a celebrity speaker? You said you know some famous personalities. Which one shall we approach first?"

"I know them, yes, but that was because they supported NCF. You're going to have to tell me who will support prisoner counselling. It's not everyone's cup of tea, is it?" I was getting near the edge of my patience at that point. "I don't know but I am asking you to start doing some research. I have to go to meetings all afternoon and you can stop the data entry for a few hours while you investigate."

"How am I going to do that? You'd better tell me which of the people who came to your previous events is high net-worth."

Here we go again round the same circle. You can't raise money unless you have people who are willing to give you money. You can't get people to give you money unless they already have. No. That can't be true. Otherwise my fund raiser is just an administrator and certainly does not deserve to be paid more than all the rest of the staff except me. I couldn't see how to get across to Lana just how much I disagreed with her position while still remaining generally supportive as I wished to be. I thought to myself that she must have talent in this field. The Trustees were convinced that she could deliver and if she did not they would probably blame me for poor management.

I thought about my position with the Trustees. The most difficult one was Lady Young-Talbot. Her husband had been knighted for services to industry and she was very aware of the status that her title conveyed. It was best to be aware of this and to treat her accordingly. I had not discovered at that point just how important that was. Perhaps I was still smarting from the snobbery that I had encountered at my college and as a result I was not willing to bow and scrape before aristocracy either of birth or of appointment. I don't think I was actually rude but I usually addressed her as Ruth, which was actually her name, and I made sure that she was listed in the Minutes as Ruth Young-Talbot but I suppose that was partly because of my envy of her position and irritation with her superior manner. In fact I decreed that none of the Trustees should have a title in any of our written documents and, as well as respecting our Equal Opportunities Policy, I know that somewhere deep down was my determination that she should be treated as only a human being. As far as we were concerned, respect would be earned only by merit.

I had to report to the next BOT meeting on the progress of the fundraising, as well as the general financial situation. I had to do this every month and I hated it. Places were marked by copies of the papers round a long table in one of our bigger rooms. Lady YT was variable in meetings. She could be charming, smiling a mirthless, seductive smile which she rarely wasted on women but would flash at Marcus and Richard. I was not sure how she would take the news of the difficulties I was having with Lana. She would probably be pleased that I was not having any success. But perhaps that was unfair and she cared more for our charity than for petty triumphs.

Lady YT usually made a play for one of the men. Marcus and Richard often arrived together and would then sit next to each other. There was usually a wait while late comers arrived and, Marcus, the Chairman, whose office was just down the road, was the last to arrive. Rowena the drama queen, who was also a Trustee of the Bradford City School of Drama, came in with her beautiful red and gold Indian scarf knotted elegantly round her shoulders. She was greeted effusively by Lady YT who graciously invited her to sit down. I found the greeting on my lips was too late as Rowena was already talking to George the retired Head Master.

Martin, who was the vicar of an Anglo-catholic London church ambled in, took out his laptop and began to type furiously, presumably writing his next sermon. Andy, whose name in full, I think, was Andrea, was a prison visitor and had been a social worker. She dressed like a very butch lesbian and had made a passionate speech about three meetings before about how much she valued our policy of taking on trainees without regard to their sexuality. She had no patience with Lady YT, but that did not help me much, as she didn't have much patience with anybody including me.

Lady YT took Richard's arm and the two of them spoke together in low voices, both looking at me from time to time. I hoped that I was wrong and that they were talking about the chances of Bradford City in the European Cup but I doubted it. She had started out by being pro-active, inviting all the Trustees to dinner so that they could discuss how best to help with the fund-raising. She specifically told me that I would not be welcome. I know that she might have thought she would save me from an evening commitment but I took it as part of the class warfare that I was waging and that I was of a lower class because I was an employee. That sowed a seed of distrust in me which began to thrust down a root that had the power to shoot up into all my troubles at work.

After this first dinner, the Trustees began to have regular meetings over dinner and I was told about decisions that emerged from these meetings but of course had no opportunity to discuss or debate or present the staff view. There were sometimes embargoes on ideas that the senior staff had proposed and since I had no idea what the arguments were, I felt disinclined to put much effort into supporting them over these decisions. This attitude of mine was dangerous. My job should have involved supporting and mediating the decisions of the Trustees to the organisation. Because I felt excluded I didn't try very hard to do this and my downfall got closer and closer.

The next thing that happened at that fateful meeting was that Marcus arrived and called the meeting to order. Then he announced that he was going to retire from the role of Chair as of the next meeting. His firm had decided that he must go and run their new office in the Middle East. He had seen it as his duty to bring in a possible successor and the Trustees should consider the position. He then looked a bit uncomfortable and said that he would like to ask the staff who were in attendance to withdraw after the main business so that the Trustees could discuss his successor. We, the staff managers and I, looked at each other and of course, concurred. We had no choice and probably would have agreed that our absence was appropriate. What I found difficult to accept was the announcement that was made without preparation and in my eyes, we were once again excluded from important decision making and that was the only part of the statement that I really heard. I had cause to worry about the succession more than I realised. The process that they used to appoint their Chair was much less my problem than the person appointed as I later discovered.

The new chairman was a woman called Barbara Chan. She had retired from running a large national charity and had very clear ideas about how to raise money. She was often impatient and had an imperious manner that I heard had left her staff often highly indignant. At first I couldn't see what the problem was. I found her very interested in what I was trying to do. She set up regular meetings with me and for the first time in the role of CEO, I had a line manager. The first sign of trouble arose when she enquired very closely about how I was managing Lana. This was understandable as Trustees are responsible for the financial health of their organisation. I found myself confiding in her my difficulties in managing Lana. She was a great problem solver and very soon had sorted out exactly how I should be talking to Lana. I found her ideas thought provoking. "Tell her," she said "that she is still in her probationary period. Give her a financial target for the first six months." I thought that she was offering me advice as Marcus would have done in one of his infrequent telephone calls. It never occurred to me that in her view I was also in my probationary period and that I was also being given targets. She had a habit of shaking her head and then facing you with a flashing smile like a conjuror producing a triumphant rabbit. She could put a cloth over it and make it disappear again. When she did that she would stand up and make clear that the meeting was over. "I hope it goes well," she said and put her coat on. "By the way, I am assuming that you have made notes. Could you be kind enough to send me a copy?" With that she swept up her papers into her shiny briefcase and left the room. I had to go to another meeting ten minutes later and did not make the notes until the next day. I wrote down a few bullet points that I remembered all under the heading of *Barbara's suggestions* and e-mailed them straight off to her. Within an hour I had a heavily corrected version back from her. "Dear Alice, I thought I had made it clear that I expect you to carry out these actions by the next time that we meet." I wrote back that I would do what I could. To this she responded that she expected me to do what we had agreed and that she saw no reason why I could not do the whole of what she had asked.

Lana was due for a consultation with me the next day. She came in beaming. "You will be really pleased to hear this. I have been speaking to my friend who is the fund raiser for Save the Scottish Terrapin. She has the same sort of hard time that I do because she is based in London and can't seem to get much enthusiasm for Scottish terrapins. She has this brilliant arrangement of being charity of the Year. She went to talk to a big City financial business and by the time she had finished they agreed to support her charity for a whole year. We have plenty of businesses here that could afford to do that for us."

"What does *support* mean?" I asked suspiciously.

"It means that the staff make voluntary contributions. They can also do payroll giving and they will hold events for us. They might do matched funding for our Northern Marathon runners. There's no end to what they might do for us."

"So can you get that for us somewhere?"

"Of course we can. Why not?"

I noted the "we" but did not respond to it. This sounded like a really good idea. It would mean someone doing a very good presentation giving all the reasons why supporting prisoners would help them to become constructive members of society. We could appeal to the safety angle and the rehabilitation angle, detailing the recidivism figures. I was certainly willing to go and speak to anyone any time about the cause. I believed in it whole heartedly and found it easy to promote it. Even though it was Lana's job, I did think that it was my job to contribute and I was the one with the experience and expertise. "Let's think about how to go about this," I said.

"I'll make a list of companies that might be open to a presentation," she offered.

"Do it' I said. I liked to be able to be decisive."

Barbara rang me later that morning. "I believe you had a consultation with Lana today. I take it you've set her Key Performance Indicators and established her time frame." "We are embarking on a new strategy," I said rather tentatively.

"You're what? You haven't discussed any new strategy with me or with any of the Trustees I think. It is certainly our responsibility to consider and maybe approve any strategy that you would like to propose. I don't want to stand in your way or seem obstructive but we have to consider it from angles that you may not have thought of. We would be failing in our duty of care if we did not do that. At least you can have the courtesy to tell me now."

I refrained from saying that that was just what I was actually doing. I swallowed my anger and told her what Lana had told me.

"So you will be letting her off the hook just because she has come up with some new idea which doesn't involve her in actually doing her job. I shall ask you again to do as you were instructed

by me and I shall need to know that you have done so by Friday."
I was amazed and appalled. No-one had spoken to me like this for
years. In fact the only time when anyone had spoken to me like that
was when I once did a vacation job in a bank and had muddled up
some cheques that I was supposed to be counting. My mind had
wandered from the incredibly boring task and the manager came in
and shouted at me. He was very rude about people from universities who thought they knew everything and he was there to tell me
that I knew even less than the sandwich sitting on his desk. Barbara
had not ascended his heights of rhetoric but she made me feel just
as bad as he did.

After I put the phone down, I had to have a conversation with
myself about it. Should I really be asking the permission of the Trustees to do this? I tried to be impartial but it seemed to me that this
was an executive matter. There was nothing new from the point
of view of the governance of the organisation. As far as I knew,
governance did not apply to the external relations particularly.
How could I check that? I thought I was responsible for bringing
in the funding. If I wasn't and the Trustees wanted to take it over
I would be very happy. I thought I would have a talk with Marcus.
He might be able to give me a reasonable idea about what the limits
of my discretionary powers might be in practice. I rang him and to
my relief he answered and suggested that we could meet for coffee
the next morning as long as I would come to him.

I made my way through the security measures at his Bank and
was shown into his Office where he sat behind a desk so large
that I had seen the like only in American films about psychoanalysts. He wore his business suit as always and had the regulation
poppy as we were at the end of October. His hair was grey but
still thick and he looked very distinguished here in his own territory. I had not realised quite how lucky we had been to have him
as Chairman. His office had all the trappings of a man of consequence who was highly successful. But behind the desk he was
still the same kind and slightly concerned man that he had always
been.

I told him that I did not want to keep him more than a few minutes, but that I was worried because I did not fully understand how
much responsibility I should take in my role as Chief Executive of a
charity. Should I perhaps consult the Charity Commission?

"No, no," he said at once, "there's no need to get into their clutches over this. You made the mistake of calling your initiative a 'new strategy'. It is a new strategy in the common sense use of the expression but it is not a new organisational strategy. You have to make the money to cover the shortfall in the income. How you propose to do that is operational. You have to report in any detail that the Trustees choose on that but you do not have to ask first whether you can do it in this way or that way. The Trustees do have to assume that you will do it in an ethical way and that you won't bring the organisation into disrepute."

That cheered me up considerably. I did not doubt the accuracy of his knowledge and I was happy with that response. My only problem was how to deal with Barbara. She would not like being told that I had asked for advice from Marcus and she especially would not like me saying that I wanted to do things my way without consulting the BOT or at least consulting her personally over every-thing. I thought that I should not appear to be complaining about her to Marcus so I said nothing more about it but asked him how his life was going now that he was no longer spending so much of his time on helping us. He said that he missed it, and missed even the BOT meetings. He lived alone as far as we knew and had often said that he wished he had children. We knew that he had not married but I assumed that he had a mistress or some such arrangement. Perhaps you don't have a mistress unless you are married. Poor Marcus, he could not enliven his early old age with something you would call an affair unless of course he found a married woman. That might give him as much of an affair as he would want to have. I wondered momentarily why I was thinking about Marcus hav-ing an affair. I didn't think I found him attractive. Then it hit me. Who was I fooling? Of course I found him attractive. I liked him and I was interested in what he would be like as a partner. He was good looking and, as far as I knew, he was available.

So if I could be interested in another partner, so could Oliver. I put my garden fork away in the tiny space that was left in the garage for tools, right at the end of all the packing cases that we were going to unpack one day. Slowly I made my way up the path that wound through the patches of lawn that I had not yet turned into vegetable beds. I had many plans for improvement but not much action yet. Whatever the news was, Oliver would not improve from being kept waiting. He was not the most patient of men at the best of times and recently he had been verging on the irascible. I ran out of lingering time and went in to his study. He had made it his own room with the male idea of masculine black leather chairs and a pile of books overflowing onto the floor from the substantial desk that we had found in a shop that was definitely second hand rather than antique. It had looked out of place in among all the pine and plywood and he had immediately fastened on it as the desk that would enable him to produce good work. It was piled high with papers and note books. He had no secretary at hand and he never did any filing on his own. I sat down in the only chair that had no papers on its seat and waited. He came round from his desk and sat in the other chair. He seemed in no hurry to get to the point either. "What's the matter?" I asked in despair.

"You know that I went for a check-up last week." I nodded, suddenly very frightened. "They were giving me the results of some tests. They have told me that I have a small tumour. It's operable of course and I shall be fine. I just thought I had better tell you."

I sat frozen to the spot. *What* was he telling me? I knew that he found it very difficult to tell me anything about his health. He was determined that I would not have an opportunity to make a fuss. His mother was a great fusser. She was a strong woman who should have run a large company herself, but, being born when she was, all she ran was a family. Oliver was the oldest of three boys and because he had asthma, she had become very protective of him. He could not bear being "delicate" and needing an inhaler and he could not bear a woman to take charge of him. I had managed to stay with him by refusing to try to look after him. I assumed that he knew what his body needed and that he would look after himself if he had an asthma attack. They had got less frequent anyway. I liked to think that the truth that men are healthier if they are married (on average) was being demonstrated by his general good health and success. In an instant he had terrified me with the use of the word *cancer*. My mind buzzed with questions and with the problem of what I could ask and how I could ask it. The first question burst out of me even before he had finished speaking and if there was one thing that annoyed him more than another, it was being interrupted. "You are having an operation?" I wanted to know when, what would they do, what had they said to him. I also wanted to know who was talking to him. Had he just been to see the GP or was there someone more like an oncologist or a urologist or whoever was appropriate for this area of a man's body?

He fiddled with his pen. "Yes. All I know is that they are putting me on the waiting list. I don't know how long that is likely to take. I have an appointment with the consultant in the middle of next month."

"You can't wait that long. We will have to get you seen privately," I found myself saying. It came out aggressively because I was expecting him to argue. When he merely said we could look into it, I realised just how frightened he was too. I got up from my chair and went and put my arms round him. "We will do it. We will get you the best treatment there is."

"You have to recognise that it costs a lot of money to get private treatment. A consultation is one thing but I don't think we can afford the operation."

At that moment there was nothing that would have stopped me from getting him the private treatment that he needed. I would make it happen. I had no doubt at all that I could make it happen.

We didn't have much money in the Bank as cash but I knew that Oliver had kept investments so that they would provide us with an income and would not risk losing the capital that we were investing. I knew this as background but did not want to start talking about it then. I just wanted to know what Oliver knew about his condition. I wanted to know that he would be all right. I wanted to know what he knew.

Margaret nodded at this. "Yes, we all suffer from wanting to know so that we can have some sort of control." Alice heaved a sigh. "I thought it was just me" she said. The sense of relief lasted until she found herself out in the road on the way back to the bus stop. What was that about? She didn't say anything new. She didn't even tell me how much it will cost and I can't afford much. Alice realised that she was going to have to work hard at this therapy with this therapist but there was something about talking to her that made her want to go back.

The cost began to worry Alice. She decided that she must find out whether she could really afford to be doing this. She was dreading both asking the question and hearing the answer. Rosalie had said that fees were very important and she would have to find the money somehow or she would not be able to continue. The best solution to all problems was to look at some websites. They were all very cagey about fees and just said that a fee would be discussed. This put Alice into a state of severe anxiety: Why had Margaret not discussed it? Was she feeling sorry for her? Or was she just going to land it on her after she had already incurred a debt? All the warm feelings she had taken away from the last session melted away and she began to feel suspicious that Margaret could not be a good therapist after all.

Alice began the next session by saying "You haven't told me how much I will have to pay." She tried to sound neutral but she realised that her doubt and anxiety came across as accusing.

"How much do you think you should pay?"

Alice stared at her. Could Margaret seriously be asking her to set her own fee? The silence went on long enough to become uncomfortable. Then Margaret put her head on one side, "That means something to you?" "Yes," said Alice sadly It reminds me of my mother." She was not sure that she wanted to tell Margaret what she was thinking but decided that she had nothing to lose now:

> I was thinking of my mother. She would give me my pocket money—sixpence a week and would say: what do you think you might spend it on this week? I always felt that I should say I would save it. She liked to tell me about her own parents who were always very short of money. My grandfather was a doctor in a northern mining town and his patients never paid him. So Granny used to have difficulty finding any money for anything but he wouldn't press his patients who were miners who were often poor. Granny took me to see some of the miner's widows. They were still mourning their men who had died in an explosion. The miners looked after each other as best they could but food was a priority and dentist's; fees were just impossible to find. Granny saw their struggles and she learnt the importance and fragility of security. She used to say "If you want something, it's worth saving up for it." I usually only wanted to buy a few pence worth of sherbet from Woolworths. It was lemony and kind of fizzy and we ate it out of a paper bag by sticking a finger in and licking it off the finger. It didn't seem very worthy of Mum or Granny to spend the hard earned sixpence on things like that. So my immediate reaction to

Margaret's question was shame. I knew I could get this wrong. But I was already worried about money. If I had to manage without Oliver, I would need to conserve all the money I had. I did a quick consideration yet again of how much money I had. It wasn't going to be different but I just wanted to feel the comfort of thinking: yes, I have ten thousand pounds in my savings account. Oliver had said that I ought to buy some shares or one of the government savings plans: a Tessa or an Isa or something. I hadn't done that and now perhaps he was not well enough to do it for me as he always would have done. Still I had the money and it was earning a little bit of interest.

I also had a little income of my own from my job with the Open University. It was a little regular cheque at the end of each month but sometimes when I had marked some assignments or exam papers I could put in a big claim and then the cheque that would come would be substantial. I loved those months when I felt that I had contributed a large amount to our income. My visits to the town centre always included a few minutes outside the Bank checking our balance. I knew how much there ought to be at each point in the month and if there were less, I would get really worried. What I liked best was to go there at the beginning of the month, just after any income was credited and before the mortgage and standing orders were taken out. Just for a day or two it looked as though we were comfortable. Then it would all crumble away and I would be left trying to manage on less than we needed, keeping the grocery bills as low as possible. In those days I used to buy what we needed nearly every day in the village at the bottom of the hill. Shopping once a week at the supermarket after it opened was much better from the point of view of controlling the budget, but while the children were small I needed the pretext to get out of the house at least once a day. It gave a shape to the day and I might meet someone who would make me feel human again. I didn't dislike spending time with the children but I felt the lack of adult company and someone to talk to especially when Oliver went away overseas and left me with a baby of three months and a toddler of two and a half. I discovered then just how much I needed the time in the evening when there were a few precious hours to sit by the fire and read or maybe even talk to each other.

Margaret seemed to understand this. She just raised her eyebrows a little and nodded. "Sometimes money feels like power and the lack of it feels like helplessness."

Alice pondered over *helplessness* on the way to the bus stop. She knew that she had felt frustrated and depressed before she had found this full time job. Perhaps that was it. She had felt more powerful when she found a job but was it because of the money? She did not like to think so but could not completely deny it. She's right. Money matters, thought Alice.

CHAPTER TWO

Adrift without a compass

"I'd better begin nearer the beginning" Alice said. And began the story that went on for many sessions, because she found that she enjoyed telling it and she began to realise that she wanted to hear it herself.

I was born in my grandparents' house in a small town further north. It was a mining village with streets of small terraced houses with back yards that are familiar now in films like *Billy Elliot*. My grandparents stayed in their house where Grandad also had his doctor's surgery and, although my parents moved us to very different surroundings, I remember the smell of coal fires and the cracks in the footpaths in those depressing streets. Yet now I come to think of it the streets were not depressing to me then. I skipped over the cracks as Granny took me to the playground. I must have been about four when I first became aware of the joys of Granny's playground. There was a huge slide which took all my courage to climb. There were boys there, urchins with torn short trousers and full, rich Geordie accents, or rather dialects. I spoke "posh" and wore skirts as little girls did. They threatened to push me off the top step just as I launched myself onto the terrifying shining path that would take me safely back to the ground. I loved it there. Maybe even the sense of danger was part of the attraction.

My main memory is that I was different and I suffered for it. My parents rented a big old house that had belonged to the church commissioners. I don't know why the Church had acquired it because it was nowhere near a church. Perhaps that was why it ceased to be useful to them. It was in need of care and my parents undertook to care for it. We all cared for it. I and my two little sisters had to help to tame the huge garden. My father worked all the time and my image of him now is of someone wearing old corduroy trousers digging or trundling a heavy old wheelbarrow. He began to grow everything then because money was always a problem. He had a day office job in the local authority. I'm not sure what exactly he did but I know he didn't enjoy it and he was clearly not very high up the hierarchy. What he loved was to come home and change into his old gardening clothes and get outside. He was a gentle man and animals and birds loved him. We had a dog, a black collie/terrier cross called Perkin who was wild and badly behaved and male, and a sedate female cat called Wink who was clearly outraged by the behaviour that Perkin could get away with.

I remember that things happened to me rather than that I made things happen. After some mysterious conversations between our parents in which there was mention of "where to put them" which worried us a bit in case it related to us, I and my sister were gathered into the back of the old Morris and the whole family drove to a farm where we collected six Light Sussex hens crossed with Rhode Island Reds. They were in a big crate which was loaded into the back of the car because it wouldn't go into the boot. My little sister and I squeezed onto the seat beside them, awed by their anxious clucking and worried by the smell and the obviously uncontrolled excreting that they were doing. When we got them home we discovered the plan, which was that they would live in the old potting shed. Although I was only about eight, I was proud to be put in charge of feeding them in the mornings with the mixture of grain and mashed up shell in the big sacks in another of the outhouses. I loved the feeling of scattering the grain on the floor of the henhouse and the way the chickens would cluck with delight and patter about looking for the precious grains. I like the way it ran through my fingers. I wasn't so keen on raking out the foul straw and putting the clean straw on the floor which I had to do as well. Yet I found that I didn't want to give the job to my sister. Perhaps I just enjoyed the cleanness after I swept up. I couldn't have actually liked the mess, could I? There was a very distinctive smell in the hens' droppings which is different from that of any other form of manure. I found them disgusting but fascinating and I think I always cared about them because they needed me and because I had witnessed their anguish on being taken away from what I assumed had felt like home to them.

Alice paused in her narrative and looked at Margaret instead of out of the window. Why was she telling her that? She had got into a kind of daze and had just transported herself back to the place she had loved. Then all of a sudden she was back in the room with a stranger. Margaret had stirred and had jolted Alice back to the present.

"We have to stop in a few minutes and we need to decide whether you want to continue," Margaret said. "Yes of course I do," Alice snapped, "I've only just begun."

"Very well then. The same time next week."

During that week Alice worried more about Oliver than she had before. She found herself visualising Oliver and his wan sick face as he said, "I'm all right. Don't fuss."

The irony was that I hadn't worried about cancer before he broke the news to me. I noticed that he got up in the night to pee more that he had before but I just thought that all men tended to get that way as they got older. It didn't mean that they were ill. What I was worrying about was his drinking. He had always enjoyed good wine and we both drank more than was good for us at College. We had a group of friends and we went to pubs and drank pints, limited only by our lack of money. Later we began to think that we could afford to drink wine. I didn't want any alcohol when I was pregnant and had drunk only small quantities since then. Oliver had discovered that his colleagues in the Institute preferred wine to beer and they drank red wine in quantities that seemed similar to the pints that they had all drunk as undergraduates. I was worried that his drinking would damage his liver but I never thought of the possibility of cancer at 37.

We are both the same age and we met in our second year at University. We met at a party of course. I had a friend who was reading physics and she met Oliver at a lecture where he had immediately invited her to a party. My friend Jeanne was very beautiful. She seemed to have taken to me when we met at the Reception for freshers in our first day at our women's college. Perhaps at some level she felt that I set off her golden beauty to perfection. I think I did. I was not beautiful even then although there is always some benefit from being young. I had light brown hair and glasses. My mother had been very protective and warned me against the dangers of young men. She had no idea what to expect from a college, but she was not wrong in imagining that there would be plenty of young men wanting sex. In those days the ratio of women to men was about 1 to 10 and there were only a few colleges that women could attend so we were quite a rare commodity.

Being in a women's college out of the city centre tended to nullify that advantage, in that by the time I cycled back from a lecture and spent a few hours in the college library, I and my two really close friends tended to go and make coffee and drink it in our rooms. We usually congregated in Jeanne's room because it was on a corner and seemed a little bigger than ours. It had just the same furniture though, a narrow hard single bed and one arm chair and one desk. We brought our own cushions and sat on the floor as well as on the bed. Our other good friend was Elsie. She had a huge collection of jazz records and her brother was a trumpeter. We had all been at schools where music lessons meant singing and the only other instrument on offer was piano and that at my school was an "extra." I would not have dreamed of asking for money for an "extra." I don't think I ever contemplated it. I just knew that it was out of the question. So knowing that Elsie's brother had got himself a paper round and gone out and suffered through rain, cold and early mornings to pay for a trumpet and then lessons with a local musician seemed impossibly creative and brave. Some of his achievement rubbed off on Elsie. She had been to one of the few co-educational grammar schools that existed then and she also knew boys or "men" as we were beginning to call them. I went to the city with her to see where things were. We tied up our bikes with the cumbersome chains and padlocks that we had been advised to use and wandered round one of the many book shops.

We had a long reading list each for our respective subjects and were wondering whether we could afford to buy any of the texts. I had to decide how to spend my grant because I was quite sure that I could not ask my parents for any more money. Maybe I would just buy the text book with the passages that needed to be translated.

Elsie's parents were clearly much worse off than mine. Her father worked in a garage as a forecourt assistant and her mother had worked part time in a shop but had asthma and found that the dust was too much for her. She stayed at home and fretted about her inability to help her two children enough. The income that they managed to bring in was marginally enough to survive on in their two up and two down council house. The good thing was that Elsie got the maximum grant and was going to be able to buy all the books on her list if she wanted to. I saw with surprise that she couldn't or wouldn't buy them because she simply never went into a shop and just bought what she needed. She bought the cheapest one only and seemed distressed about that. For the first time, I was in close contact with someone who had the sort of money to spend that my friends at school had, but was so conditioned to poverty that she couldn't spend money at all. It took me a while to understand her difficulty. In fact I didn't really understand it until I went to stay with her in the vacation and saw her mother's thin, pinched face and her father's perpetually anxious expression as they sat at the small table by the kitchen fire, cutting thin slices off a loaf and eating the bread with margarine and no jam. I began to realise that I had an attitude to money. What I felt and what I did was not inevitable but had a reason and a root in the past.

Jeanne was much more like my friends at school. Her parents were both academics and money had not been a problem for her at school. She had long auburn hair and she had a habit of tossing it as if to clear her mind as well as the hair out of her eyes. She wasn't aware that she was doing it but somehow it set off her green eyes, which even I could see, were large and brilliant. Oliver was enthralled at once but he hadn't a hope. She already had met Noel who was an actor and took the leading role in the main University drama production for that year which was to be Chekhov's *Uncle Vanya*. Jeanne took me along to Oliver's party and there he was made aware that she was willing to be friendly but that was as far as it was going. He turned to me and we retired to a corner and he told me all about his interest in film and jazz, both of which were areas that I was only just beginning to appreciate. I was an enthralled and eager acolyte and I think he must have enjoyed my willingness to look up to him as someone who knew so much more than I did.

It was getting near the time to stop the session and Alice knew that she had to say something about fees to Margaret.

"How about £20 per session?" she asked tentatively.

"If you can manage that and not have to stop because of money, that will be fine," Margaret said. Alice's first feeling was great relief. She should be able to manage that sort of payment and it would not make a huge difference to her finances even if she had to find the money for Oliver's private treatment. "Thank you" she said. Margaret just smiled. Alice got the impression that she was putting up with that response and on the way home she began to replay the scene in her mind. Margaret became more and more accusing with each run through. "You idiot," Alice told herself. "She thinks you know what the usual fee is and it's probably far more than that. My only hope is to ask Rosalie straight away what she was paying. Why on earth have I not done that before?" Alice felt a complete idiot and was sure that she could not go back.

As the week went by Alice passed through shame and humiliation and then reached a point where she was feeling that she wanted to shout aloud that it was not her fault. She didn't know how to play this game. So how could she be blamed if she didn't get it right? Then she managed to say to herself. This is ridiculous. You're having a conversation with someone in your own head. She can't answer and it would be better if you knew what she would really say. So go and tell her. She found some sort of courage out of her desire to shout at Margaret and did go back. Margaret sat and waited for her to begin as usual.

"I've been very worried this week" Alice began after a long silence. Margaret raised her eyebrows. "I wish you would help me sometimes," Alice burst out and then stopped. That was very unlike her. "I don't really know what came over me." I like to keep things friendly and I would not normally let anyone see it even if I was really angry. Of course in this case I wasn't really angry, just a bit unsettled.

Margaret looked at her steadily and said "Your own idea about what you should pay seems to have upset you."

"No," Alice said, "it's not exactly that. It's more that I don't know what you are thinking about it. You are not giving me any land marks. It's like being adrift in a rowing boat without any oars. No, not without oars, without a compass."

"So you're upset because you think I might not approve of what you offered, even though I asked you to say."

At this point Margaret must have been aware that Alice was really angry although all she did was burst into tears. They were tears that Alice herself didn't understand. Why should being angry make her cry? She felt shamed and humiliated by the whole situation. Margaret leant forward in her chair and said very gently "I think this has reminded you of something."

Alice replied immediately that it did not: "I don't think so." Then she realised that in fact it did.

It reminded me of how I felt when I heard my mother discussing with my father the need to bring my grandparents to live with us. It was nine o'clock and I had been in bed for an hour and a half but it was a summer evening and the sky was still light. I couldn't get to sleep and when I heard Big Ben striking for the nine o'clock news on the wireless, I crept downstairs to tell my mother that I couldn't sleep. I suppose I was about eight at the time. When I was outside the door I paused because although the news was on, my mother was talking and her voice was strained and anxious. "I don't know how we'll manage if we don't. We have to move and how can we buy anything without any capital? It won't be easy but they can bring their money from the sale of their house and get us started."

I had no idea what she was talking about but I could tell that she was anxious. I wanted to rush in and tell her that it would be all right, but as I didn't know what was going on, there was nothing I could do. Anyway I should not have been listening. I crept back upstairs and lay weeping under the covers. I recognised that mixture of guilt, anxiety and concern. Then I thought, a bit more reasonably that I could not be concerned about Margaret or only in a very general way. I hardly knew her so I should pull myself together and get my priorities straight. I didn't tell her any of these thoughts so there was rather a long silence. She just sat and waited so I thought "well you can just wait then. If you won't ever help me, I'm not going to bother to talk to you. I suppose I just sat and sulked and Margaret said nothing until the end when she just said the usual "It's time." Alice stalked off, now just angry, not sad any more: I didn't understand how she could leave me to struggle in this way. I could not believe that she didn't know how unhappy I was. So she must know and was just taking no notice. She was probably thinking about her next meal. Then it dawned on me that something all these events had in common was that I found it upsetting when I didn't know what someone was thinking. Why did I care? I was wanting to give them something but was prevented by my ignorance, my pathetic, annoying ignorance.

I went home and found another place where ignorance was painful to me.

Oliver's diagnosis had been confirmed. He was now waiting to hear about the treatment that would be available on the NHS. He had wanted to go to his appointment at the hospital on his own. I had been desperately keen to go with him to find out what was happening but I could see that it was important to him that he had control over something so I swallowed my anxiety and waited for him to come back.

When he opened the front door, I dropped the book I was trying to read and rushed to meet him. He came and sat down beside me and said nothing. I recognised that feeling of not knowing how to start so I offered him a drink. When I had got us glasses of his current favourite red wine, he told me a little.

"Mr Mahmoud was not available so I saw his registrar. He seemed nice enough." I could tell that he was discouraged and felt cheated but I didn't know how to be helpful. "I think the Registrars know all about the latest treatments," was all I said. "Oh yes. He wants me to have hormone therapy although they haven't ruled out surgery yet. He's going to discuss it with the consultant and let me know."

I took a large mouthful of the red wine. "So what are the pros and cons of those? I've never heard of hormone therapy. What is it?" I was almost unable to speak and I think what came out sounded objective and uninvolved. I could have wished to be uninvolved but could never have achieved that. It was the last thing I felt, but I know it came across to Oliver as if I didn't really care. I cared profoundly but my voice wouldn't do what I wanted it to. He shut down and from then on he has not told me much. I am left with searching websites and trying to find out what the options are so that I can ask him what is happening and will have some idea of what it means if he ever will answer me. I am left in fear and ignorance so again, ignorance troubles me.

Alice realised on the top deck of the bus going home that she was choosing carefully what to say. Unless she could begin to talk fully again, this would be a waste of precious money. What if he needed it for treatment, What if he died and she needed money to live?

The next week Alice sat down and gazed out of the window. Today she would tell Margaret her how she felt honestly:

> I remembered going up to the attic at the big house where we lived. The attics ran the whole length of the house and formed a series of small rooms with sky lights. They were all empty. My parents had not put anything up there so the rooms were available for us to play. In broad daylight I was happy to go up there and be in a world without adults, but when it began to get dark the attics were places of fear: rustlings and creakings that must have gone on in the daylight too but seemed acceptable in the hot dusty emptiness of the day lit rooms. My best friend came to play and we found the place perfect for the meetings of our secret society. I sometimes allowed my little sister to enter the stronghold made with a few cardboard boxes and two cushions that I had found in the store room. The main idea of the society was to keep other people out so it never got further than a list of rules:
>
> - No-one can belong unless we say they can.
> - Everyone has to bring two biscuits to the meetings. Some people can bring two gooseberries instead if we agree.
> - The password is "snowdrop."

When Margaret heard about the rules, she stirred slightly and said "Have you kept to the rules?" Alice thought about that.

> I suppose I have. There is a sort of fortress and I have not let people in. Perhaps the criteria have moved on from two biscuits but I can see that people have to bring something. That was an early

understanding of some sort of law of quid pro quo. My friend, Hilary, and I thought we had something to offer, I suppose, although of course looking back now I can see that we were just imitating the world of adults. I was more aware of prices and demands than I would like my own children to be. Our currency was biscuits which were in short supply because they were controlled by the adults but we also found a currency of berries. We particularly liked the sweet gooseberries because they didn't squash so easily and we could carry them around in our pockets. So even then I suppose we realised that you can create your own currency which is not the standard one of coins and notes. It all depends what you can get with your money.

Alice paused in her self-analysis because Margaret was looking bored. Alice realised that what she was not talking about was the rule about not letting people in. "Are you asking me about not letting people in?" she said lamely. "I think you might be asking yourself," was the only reply. Alice did not like the way in which Margaret handed things back to her. It made them stay with her and she knew she would find herself asking the question during the week. Did she shut people out?

After mulling this over during the week, Alice marched in and began immediately to say to Margaret:

"I don't know whether I shut people out but in any case I want to tell you about Oliver's treatment and the question about whether he should have hormone treatment. And," she added, "how I will pay for it?" Margaret looked bored again. "Is that the most important thing?" Suddenly Alice was furious again. How dared she tell her what to talk about? How dared she not want to hear? Alice could hardly look at her and just got up and left. That was the first time she had ever left before the end of a session. She stormed up the road and a bus was coming so she leapt onto it. Then she began to think about what she had done and how she would ever get out of it.

CHAPTER THREE

Running up debts

Alice spent a week obsessively thinking about how angry she was and how outrageous Margaret's behaviour had been. Oliver hardly spoke to her and she didn't try to get him to talk. She thought she could find out what she needed to know from the websites but what she really needed to know was that the treatment would work for him. She was caught in the not unusual trap of feeling that she couldn't live with him but she certainly could not live without him. He sat in his study and she spent a lot of time in the garden ferociously pulling out weeds one at a time and making ugly little piles of earth with a few weeds and also some bulbs and a few periwinkles. These were supposed to be making ground cover and keeping the weeds out but they were thin and had not got any kind of a grip before the weeds had spread in a glorious riot of dandelions, buttercups, and brambles. She got hot and angry and began to throw the weeds into a pile on the path with the result that there was a mess of earth all over the path and a mess of bits of weed all over the presumptive vegetable patch. Nothing will ever grow here except weeds she stormed to herself but she stayed there and went on scratching at the hard, dry earth.

When Thursday came, Alice got on the bus in a daze. She didn't stop to think about whether she wanted to go back. She just went. Margaret opened the door just as usual, gave a brief smile, just as usual. Alice sat down feeling like a small child who has done something very silly. She would have given a lot for Margaret to have said something at the beginning, just to know what she was thinking. After an uncomfortable silence she began to ask herself why she didn't ask her. "Are you angry?" she managed.

"No," Margaret said, "but I think you might be."

"I was," Alice acknowledged, "but now I'm just upset." She hadn't intended to say that. But then, she thought, how much of what I say is really intended or planned?

"You are dealing with a lot that is upsetting," Margaret said. She said just that but she said it so gently that Alice started to cry and wept uncontrollably for about ten minutes. Margaret didn't move but there was something about her waiting that was different. Gradually Alice descended into snuffling and blowing her nose and realised that she was going to feel better now.

There was still the question of why Margaret had seemed bored and didn't seem to want to hear what Alice obviously wanted to talk about. Alice looked carefully at her. She looked back steadily and didn't smile but seemed to be encouraging Alice to say what was in her mind.

"I was very upset," she said, "because you didn't want to hear what I wanted to tell you."

"And you can't see why?"

"Exactly. I can't see why."

"I might be wrong, but I thought you were going to go on filling the whole time with Oliver."

"So, everything depends on what you want."

"Has that been your experience so far?"

Alice paused. No, it had not been her experience at all but she wanted to be angry. She was not yet ready to give up but she was ready to stop showing her feelings. "You win," she said and could see that she had an impact with that. All Margaret said was "I didn't realise there was a contest." "Not a contest, a battle", Alice said and immediately regretted it. Margaret hadn't deserved that. She wanted to escape. "I think we need to make a new start for today," Margaret said, echoing that thought.

Alice had begun to realise that she could pause and think before launching into any more attacks. So she looked out of the window and watched a small brown bird wandering about on the path investigating small cracks where there just might be an ant. "I don't need to find ants," she thought. "I had better get back to what I came for." She still didn't really understand what she had done that Margaret wouldn't tolerate but the safe thing to do was to go back to the story. Maybe she would just come once a fortnight or even once a month. That would ease the financial problem. Then she realised that she could not leave the gaps that long. Even when she was most angry she had to come back and say so. There was also the story to tell. If Margaret would come with her that would be good but she was going there anyway.

The house was always a refuge from the other children who teased me about my accent or my school uniform. Once through the front door I was safe. I think I wanted to get inside somewhere and shut the door. I want to tell you more about our life inside the old house. I was about ten when we moved there and I loved it. What we had there was space and all sorts of possibilities. The garden was huge and had a large wild area that was called the "tennis court" and you could see that it was about the size of a tennis court and no doubt there had been a gracious era when I imagine that young men and girls dressed in very respectable tennis whites sat under the trees and had afternoon tea after a game. There was a strip of woodland and some steps down to another equally large grassy area that was called the "swimming pool". If it had ever been a swimming pool it must have been very big and must have taken a great deal of care to keep it clean. There was no evidence of any kind of heating and I suppose that the sun was the only heat source. Open air, unheated swimming pools were rare for obvious reasons so this garden was quite unique in my experience but I never really doubted that it had been a swimming pool and that my tennis girls had put on voluminous swimming costumes on lovely summer days and lounged by the pool.

There were many outhouses in the garden too with names that suggested a small home farm. We made the pig sty into a house for our imaginary play as it was as far away from the house as you could get and that gave us the opportunity of imagining that adults were not in charge of us as they were out of sight and out of earshot. I glanced at Margaret but she still seemed to be listening. There was a stable and numerous potting sheds. One big green house had an old vine growing across the end wall and there was a flue for heating it from an old fireplace in a shed behind.

The whole place was reminiscent of past grandeur but with a sense of something that was so well lost that it could never be found again. I knew that my parents were struggling to manage the house. My father had no-one to help him in the garden but me, and I felt a constant sense of guilt because I didn't try hard enough. I didn't enjoy gardening except for a few very specific tasks like planting peas. I liked helping to unwind the string to make a straight row and then digging out a shallow trench. I liked putting in the peas in a zigzag pattern and finally covering them up in a reassuring way with the softest, most friable earth, warm and moist and dark. The old dried up peas that we planted would produce strong green plants and in their turn they would bear more peas. But those peas would be delicate and as sweet to the taste as any child could wish. In the garden the only rules were set by my father. He told me how to plant and how to care for the young plants and how to harvest the fruit and the vegetables. There was no limit put on consumption either because the garden was so big and prolific. We picked and gathered and preserved and my parents were able to give away to my grandparents and to their friends some of the bounty. I was proud when that time of year came round and other people would admire what my father had managed to grow. I was implicated in the pride because I was his main assistant even though I knew I was often grudging and reluctant and could have done much more. He never made me feel guilty although there were times when he put his foot down and said that I must help because the potatoes would sprout if we didn't dig the patch and get them planted. So with a bad grace I would leave my little plastic dolls in their shoe box hospital and put my boots on so that I could go out and dig. Once I was out there, I usually discovered some exhilaration in being able to slam my good sharp spade into the ground and turn over a spoonful of earth, just me and my father next to each other under the sky.

I didn't experience failure very much then. That waited for me. That is not to say that I was always happy or content. Far from it. I was humiliated by the little streetwise kids who lived on the council estate at the bottom of our drive. They waited for me to come to the bus stop every morning in my school uniform, all green and bought at great expense from the department store that was the only stockist. Then until the bus came, they would torment me, throwing sticks at me from just far enough away for me not to be able to see them clearly. They probably realised that because I wore glasses I couldn't see them well; they shouted "Goggle eyes!" at me and threatened to break my glasses. I was very worried about that because I knew that my parents had gone to a lot of trouble to get them for me. I did not realise that they were paid for by the National Health Service (which had just begun to operate) and I would have been very relieved if I had known that my tormentors did not have the power to hurt my parents as well as me. As it was, I never said anything to anyone and just gripped my satchel and my hat grimly, willing the bus to come.

School was a refuge like the house. Since all the other children were wearing the uniform and were being treated by the staff as though we were social equals, there was less stress, only the usual questions about who was whose friend and who was the alpha female.

I was not the alpha female. Emily was the unquestioned leader who didn't have to exert herself at all. She simply sat on the wall and her court gathered round her, waiting to hear what we should play that day. The important thing was to be one of her courtiers. If you were not, you were consigned to a lonely lunch hour in which you had to go and sit on the grass by yourself and hope that someone else might be equally lonely and come and talk to you. The trouble was that once you committed yourself to being in Emily's court, you did not have access to any of the smaller, less glamorous courts and if you were thrown out of it on a whim, which was how the thing worked; you had to hope for mercy.

I remember the handstand game. Emily sat on the grass for this and announced "Scissors" whereupon about eight little girls would all attempt a handstand with a scissor leg motion. She would then decide who had produced the best scissors. That fortunate one could get a point and when you had five points you could take over as the judge for a while. I don't remember ever being the judge. I was mostly happy to be allowed to compete.

I found the sports field more humiliating. I was a plump little child and hated having to do gym and games in green school knickers and a yellow aertex blouse. I had decided that I was very bad at everything in gym and maybe I just gave up and didn't really try. Games weren't quite as bad. I enjoyed Netball and was quite good at hurling myself about the pitch and could always see the ball and knew exactly where it was. I was pretty bad at tennis, partly because I couldn't see the ball until it had landed on my side of the net which was a bit late for making any kind of policy decision about what to do. I could never quite get up the interest in running up and down the field to be any good at hockey. In that whole area I embraced failure and joined those who skulked in the library whenever possible rather than go to gym or games.

I did not write myself off as a complete failure until much later on. I did well at school academically and that was my comfort and my solace. I actually liked to do the work. I was interested in everything except for maths. Maths must have been too close to what my father wanted for me. He wanted a son and he wanted a physicist. I was never going to be either. Knowing this made me so nervous about maths and sciences that I did least well in those subjects and had a wonderful time in the arts subjects where I did manage to come top in those competitive days when there was still such a thing as a class list and even later on a year-list read out on the last day of term by the headmistress to the whole school. Each girl had an average in the exams and was placed in order and the list was read from bottom to top so much like the judging of a television talent contest, there was a long wait to hear which of the three or four of us who were in the running had actually come top of the girls in our year. I came top once but mostly I just missed it to because my best friend Eleanor was better than me at maths and sciences. That was not a failure. My first real failure came in the sixth form when we had dances with the sixth forms of boys' schools. I had no contact with boys in my family and my only knowledge of what boys might be like came from the urchins who attended my route to and from school. So I can see now that I was nervous of them as if they were horses. They can kick and they can bite. This attitude fitted well with my mother's anxiety that she repeated many times that boys should be friends and not "boy friends" until you were ready to get married. How this transition might ever take place was a mystery. As a result, I was not practised in any of the arts of seduction and kept away from places where I might have to encounter a boy. I didn't go to the dancing classes that were arranged with the boys' grammar school sixth form a few months before the Dance. Most of my friends did go and had partners already before the Dance. I went to it cold and full of trepidation.

There was also the question of the dress. My mother did her best but she could not have been expected to know what an acceptable dress would look like. The result was that I had a green dress with a giant pattern on it in a length that came down to below my knees and was about as alluring as a wet Wednesday. The result was a plain girl in a dress that her grandmother might have worn before the days when that was a fashion statement peering anxiously at the row of boys on the chairs at the opposite side of the room. That could not be and clearly was not enticing to them. I was asked to dance once and the rest of the time I sat on the chair in frozen misery. I wanted to be asked and I wanted to be left alone. I wanted to be on the dance floor and I wanted to be a million miles away from the dance floor. One of the teachers who were keeping an eye on things came and sat next to me. She clearly felt sorry for me and that was the failure, the complete humiliation. From then on, I saw myself as useless, hopelessly ugly and since no prince would come, I would just have to go off and find the way to succeed on my own.

"You were pretty determined to be a failure," said Margaret. Alice stared at her in surprise. "It was the last thing I wanted. I really wanted a long-term boyfriend."

"If you couldn't have a man, you would be one." As always, Margaret's comment was startling. What she said was sometimes surprising but usually near the mark. This time, Alice felt angry again. "You think only men can be successful? You have to be a man to succeed?" She was furious that Margaret should be so far from her own broadly feminist position.

Alice sat on the bus, looking out at the moors, and the session replayed itself. "She is supposed to think like me," she thought, "and usually I can keep up the illusion that she does when she doesn't speak and doesn't make me see otherwise. She said nothing so I went on in the hope that I could deal with it somehow later in my own time. It really upset me that I had just told her my secret, deep anxiety about myself and she was miles away from my feelings, seeing me as some kind of macho Lesbian which is probably how the sixth form boys saw me."

Alice found to her surprise that she did not brood over her comment as much that next week as she had feared. Telling Margaret these terrible memories did seem to take the sting out of them even though she thought she wanted sympathy. What she did worry about was whether she would have the nerve to tell Margaret about the most recent and greatest failure that went along with her loss. What if Alice told her, and she just said that Alice was trying to be a man? Then she had to start thinking that maybe there was something in that. "I am very competitive. I like to fight and win" she admitted to herself. "It all depends what you mean by a 'man' of course."

Alice decided to ask Rosalie where Margaret got her ideas. Then she could read up on them too so that at least she would know what she meant. That, she thought, was the answer. Alice had always found knowledge to be the key to power and had no reason to suppose that this situation would be any different even though Margaret was not as subject to any kind of control as she would have liked.

Alice decided that she would go to the next session and just see what happened:

> I hated leaving school. In spite of any difficulties in my social life it had been the best time of my life. I had three very good friends and the whole group of us in the Arts Sixth got on well together so it felt like a safe environment. They were not mean to me when I did well academically. I think now that they thought that was my compensation. They were right. It was. The shock of arriving at University was that everyone in my college had at least as much ability as me and several people had more. In addition, many of them came from famous girls' boarding schools and had that self confidence that displayed itself as total confidence that they were right and even if they were not right they were to be admired and obeyed. I immediately took up the vacant position of admiring, humble hanger on. I discovered to my dismay that his position did not include any social contact. In Hall I was tolerated if I happened to sit next to Maria, whose father was the Spanish ambassador but I was not admitted in any sense to the circle of friends who had been at Wickham Abbey School with her.
>
> I know that this kind of snobbery was endemic in those days but I was bruised by this second layer of inadequacy that I discovered in myself. My parents' lack of money had meant that although they

struggled to send me to a private primary school, they could not afford the kind of extras even there that the other children seemed to have. I felt completely unprepared for these smart young women who knew the plays that were on in the West End, who not only knew who the artists of current interest were, but knew the artists themselves. These sorts of things excluded me more effectively than their sense that I was not one of them from my clothes and my voice. Most importantly, they knew my inadequacy as soon as the question came "Which school?" They meant "Was it Cheltenham? because if it was Wickham Abbey I would know you already"

I encountered the woman in the room next to mine on my first day. I greeted her full of enthusiasm when I met her in the hall. "Hello, I'm Alice. I think we have to go and get our gowns from the College Office. Are you coming to look for it?" "Oh, no thanks. I'm going to a friend's room."

That, together with the cold tone of voice, was all it took to make me shrink away from her and not address her again unless I had to. In fact I discovered that she was from a minor public school and was on the very outermost fringes of the In group. I suppose they were all horrified to find that there were grammar school girls there. Fortunately for me I was not the only one. We all had to buy a gown and when I found the Office, I was standing next to Elsie in the queue and she was also from a grammar school. I was delighted to find how open and friendly she was and we agreed to go to Hall together as that was the first time we would have to put on our newly acquired gowns and answer the summons of the bell which tolled every night to summon us.

As it was a women's college, we had no problems about immediate competition with men. I had no wish to be involved with men at all but Elsie and Jeanne whom we met later, both did and I was happy to go along with them. That was how I met Oliver. I discovered by going to a few lectures and classes that the university almost entirely comprised men. Sadly the proportion of public school boys versus grammar school boys was about the same as for women and they were no more amenable to talking to girls who were not particularly attractive and lacked the polish of a public school background than were the women. Since it was not fashionable to go to lectures at all, there was usually only a sprinkling of people there. I mostly sat on my own and envied those who seemed

to know each other already because they had met at the Hunt Ball.
I remember one conversation on my right at one of my first lectures
which was about a "point to point." I didn't know what a point to
point was, although I had a faint idea that it was something to do
with hunting. I thought of my father working away in our garden
and wished he was a landed gentleman with a stable full of horses.
That treachery makes me cry now.

I stopped and snuffled a bit. Margaret waited.

I did a lot of things that I'm ashamed of but the thoughts now
are the hardest to bear. Maybe I'll come to that later.

For now, it's enough that I did all right in my degree. Not bril-
liantly but all right. And then I got a job. That was the first mistake. I should have done some sort of vocational training. Jeanne
was reading Philosophy, Politics and Psychology which meant that
she was going to be a psychologist. The only question for her was
how to get a clinical placement. Since her degree was good, she
found one soon enough to begin the autumn after we graduated.
Else was a lawyer and she went off to London to begin clerking.
I just thought that with a useless degree in history I had better start
to earn some money so I took a job as a junior assistant in a large
charity that was recruiting graduates, probably because they were
cheap. I could not really say that I had office skills which in those
days meant short hand and typing although I had taught myself
to type rather inaccurately but I thought I would become a manager and someone else would do the typing. In this I was more or
less right and I spent three years not unhappily in charge of donor
newsletters. I improved my typing and developed a friendly relationship with Adele, the administrator that three of us shared. She
seemed to like me and brought me slices of the exquisite cakes that
she baked and iced at weekends.

Adele liked to experiment with her baking. I think it gave her
a sense of power and independence and perhaps creativity too,
so each week there was a different flavour. Once we had liquorice
which I particularly liked. My introduction to office life was gentle.
I had a room in a tall building in the City in a house that reminded
me of the sixties film, *The L-Shaped Room* where the lonely heroine
gets her man but although there were lonely single men in the film,
I never met anyone that I liked better than Oliver. He had gone to
a Laboratory in the Midlands where he was making a name for

himself with some project on atomic theory. He also had a bleak single room and we exchanged weekends, managing to squeeze uncomfortably into the narrow, hard single beds. I suppose this was part of what precipitated us into marriage. That and my parents. I knew that they would disapprove if they knew about our lives and that for my own good they would be horrified at the idea of sex before marriage.

We had to begin to think about where and how we would live if we did get married. Oliver was a bit off hand about it. "If you want to" was his attitude. I found that less than satisfactory but I realised that it was the best I was likely to get. We decided to try and find a small flat somewhere on the outskirts of Bradford or Leeds where he was already working for his PhD and earning a little money as a lab assistant. We didn't know how we could get a car but that would be part of the plan. I realised that if we did that we would both have to travel to work and that would take up a substantial portion of our income. I heard from one of our friends that a small charity based at the far end of Marlborough Road was advertising for a Head of Training. I went for an interview in rather an ambivalent frame of mind. I had no qualifications for training people but then I had no qualifications in anything, just a degree. When I thought this way, all my repressed indignation came to the surface. Who were these people anyway? I could do the job standing on my head. The effect was evidently positive. For the first time in my life I must have seemed confident; I breezed in and didn't really care what they thought. I got the job. I didn't like the poky little offices with old, damp, smelly carpets and the cardboard walls with no sound proofing but they were prepared to pay enough to live on so I decided to put up with the premises. I had to share a small room with Anita, the Head of Befriending Services. She was a cheerful, competent woman and was pleased to see me because she had been doing my job as well as her own since my predecessor left to have a baby. "You aren't pregnant are you, Love?" she asked me, "only I couldn't bear to have to take on those training people again. They are a nightmare. They are all part time and they don't really care about us. You get one course set up and then they tell you that they have just signed a contract to teach in Poland and will not be here after all."

On my second day, I heard Anita talking to our Manager, the Chief Executive, Oswald. He tended to stay out of the way but he was talking quietly to Anita and I heard him say "Don't worry about the space. We'll make sure that you have more space next year. It'll all be different then." I hadn't been paying much attention but that did get my attention. I had been worried that she resented having me in her small office. I still thought of it as "her" office. I mulled it over for a day and eventually I told her that I had heard someone mention how difficult it was to share an office. She was immediately ready to tell me about it and at the same time she told me that Oswald would be retiring and his job would be advertised next month.

I had no feelings about Oswald one way or the other so it didn't really bother me but I could see that Anita was really upset. "No-one can replace him. He has been wonderful for us at Mental Freedom. He's taken it from being in a backwater to being part of the main-stream." I made a mental note that Anita would find it hard when Oswald left. In the meantime I got on with my job and tried to sort out the muddle that Anita had created by just having half an eye on what was happening. She was clearly aware that it was all in need of attention so I felt no need to point it out or complain to her. All I did was ask for help in understanding what was needed. She reciprocated by being as helpful as she could and never complaining when I interrupted her.

One day Anita came in from a chat with Oswald wiping her eyes. I moved my empty coffee mug off the corner of her desk and sat on it. "Whatever is the matter?" "He told me that his job was advertised in the *Guardian* last week. They will be interviewing next month and he will leave as soon as the new person can take up the post." I had realised that Oswald was gay and I was sure that Anita would know that but I didn't like to raise it. Could a single woman in her fifties be in love with a gay man, however attractive and charismatic he was?

Alice looked at Margaret who had made the characteristic small move-ment that meant that she was ready to say something. "What?" "I was wondering about your dismissal of the gay man."

"I didn't dismiss him. He was not interested in me. I wasn't inter-ested in him. I had Oliver anyway. But that isn't what you mean is it? You think I am prejudiced." She didn't agree but she didn't disagree either.

Alice realised that Margaret wanted her to think about it. Alice was beginning to understand the process. She didn't honestly think that she had any feelings about Oswald and that was not what she wanted to talk about anyway. She paused while she gave some attention to what Margaret had said. Then she found the courage to say "That wasn't the point." Alice felt a bit guilty about that: perhaps it should be the point; or at least it was *a* point.

> I really came to like and admire Anita. She had a warmth and humanity that stopped her from being self-conscious. She was open and honest and never hesitated to say what she thought was the truth however uncomfortable that might be for me or her. In short I liked her. On the bus after the session I thought about my feelings about Anita. Maybe that's what Margaret was getting at. Maybe I loved Anita. Well I did love her but how did I love her? In all honesty I did not think there was sexuality in it but more the love for a big sister. I was happy with the relationship that we had of easy but not equal friendship.
>
> The interviews came and went. The Trustees were responsible for appointing the new CEO and we were not allowed to know who the applicants were or how many there were but a week after the interviews we were summoned to Oswald's office which was slightly bigger than ours and had two small casement windows. The Chairman was sitting at the desk and Oswald was standing behind him at the window. "As you know, we have to find a replacement for Oswald. We were not able to appoint from the applicants that we had this time. The Trustees will meet to decide how to move forward at this time. Alice, would you wait here a minute please." The others left and he asked me to sit in the one chair for visitors. "If we were inviting you to apply along with two other people, would you be interested?" I was astonished. "Me? I've only just got here. I couldn't possibly do it." The response was slow but measured. "That's true and you would have to show the staff that you can have enough authority. But you have shown us, and Anita thinks you have done a very good job of sorting out the training for us. The Trustees want someone young with a good brain and some new ideas."
>
> So it was thanks to Anita, I thought. I went home in a state of panic. I could never take on the responsibility. It was too much. I told Oliver and he laughed.
>
> "Well good for you."
>
> "But I can't really do it."

"Of course you can do it. Don't be ridiculous. It's just a small charity anyway. Get out there and get on with it."

Put like that, my anxiety about the responsibility seemed a bit weak. I realised that what I was most worried about was what I had heard Oswald say several times: we are just keeping our heads above water but it is a hard time for charities. How could I keep any heads above water? I knew nothing about raising money, scarcely even knew how to read the accounts. Arthur, the Treasurer was a Trustee and he held Finance Group meetings to which I had to report on the training income and expenditure. I had managed to balance the books and achieve Mr Micawber's ideal of the annual income being just slightly above the annual expenditure resulting, as he says, in happiness. When I thought about that, I thought well maybe I could do it. Somehow it would turn out all right. I was clearly still a person who believed in glasses being half full or at least that would be so in the case of my own glass.

I applied and the Trustees appointed me. I really thought they were either not seeing what was in front of them or were hopelessly over optimistic. But there was also something in me then that would just get on with things without too much agonising. I began with gratitude to the Trustees who had enough faith in me to put me in this role so soon. The staff were not as big a problem as I had expected. I was most worried about Anita. I didn't know whether or not she had also been invited to apply for the job but if she had, she was bound to resent me, wasn't she? Surely if she had applied, she would have been appointed? I went straight to her after Oswald announced that I had been appointed as his successor. She gave me a hug and said she was delighted. I hoped she really was.

The few full time staff had all been there much longer than me but I knew that only one of them, Mike, had been invited to apply and he was quite open about it and his disappointment but he did not seem to resent me over it.

No, the staff were not the problem but the lack of money was. Even with my limited understanding of the accounts I could see that the income was about £20,000 less than the expenditure over each of the last three years. I could also see that the income in total was going down, not up. I couldn't see how the shortfall had been made up so that the accountants had allowed the organisation to go forward into the next year. This was when I started to worry seriously about my new role.

At that point I decided to speak to the Trustees about it. The chairman of the Finance Group, Arthur, would know all about it. I asked to meet with him and he was genial and pleasant as always. "Yes," he said, "we are worried about the finances and your job is to get us back onto a safe footing. What do you think you can do about it now?"

I had of course no idea but with a sort of hopeless optimism I thought that something would turn up. I thought again of Mr Micawber and wondered what happened to him in the end. Did something turn up? I had a feeling that he had emigrated to Australia and made good but I wanted to be sure. I decided to reread *David Copperfield* and find out.

CHAPTER FOUR

When do I pay?

A lice knew that she was getting near the point when she would have to look at the worst time of her life. At times, she thought, she would not be able to talk about it. Supposing Margaret did not want to hear about it. Suppose she made all the effort to face it which she knew she could do best through talking to Margaret, but what if then she felt that the talking was all wrong. Margaret had the power to do that. In fact, she had a lot of power. Alice realised that she really cared what Margaret thought. She had begun to realise that what she had felt for Anita was very much the same as what she now felt for Margaret but with one essential difference. She longed for Margaret to allow her to touch her. Alice wanted to hug her. She wanted Margaret to hug her. She tried to convince herself that she didn't feel this but she spent so much time on giving herself a good talking to that without success that she began to think she might just have to accept her feelings. So then she thought, that it might be usual. Everyone talks about falling in love with your therapist. Why should she be different? In fact she should not be different. She needed to have this experience and discover what it told her. That gave her some relief though she did worry about exactly what it did tell her.

The question that Alice then began to wonder about was how or whether this experience could be helpful. She didn't want anyone to know how she felt but she also knew that Margaret probably could see how she had changed. Perhaps, she thought, she was overwhelmed by Margaret's honesty and her unwillingness to let uncomfortable things stay hidden. Perhaps her comment about feelings about Oswald showed that she knew how Alice felt. Alice couldn't help herself. Awkward and shame-faced, Alice managed to say that she needed to tell Margaret something before she could go any further. Then she got stuck. Margaret waited exactly as Alice had known that she would. "Well, it's just that I think you know how I feel about you and it means that I am frightened to tell you any more in case you don't approve of it." Margaret spoke in her most gentle tones. "I am sorry that you have that extra demand but you know that I will listen just the same."

Alice went away to think that through. If Margaret had understood what she was talking about, she saw Alice's love for her as a demand. That was all very well and there would be demands but she had not yet actually made any. Did she think it was a demand on her to deal with Alice's feelings? Alice threw herself into a state of conflict and anxiety.

That was the week when Oliver went to see the consultant and when he came back, he said he wanted to talk. I was very pleased that he offered to talk but not happy about what he said. Apparently Mr Roberts had seen him in person this time and wanted to try a new kind of radiotherapy known as brachytherapy. This meant inserting minute radioactive pellets into the prostate at the site of the tumour. Oliver was very keen to have this because he seemed to think that it would mean he would not have to have an operation. I was very worried. For one thing it was a new treatment and I could not find much information about it on the Internet. Secondly I wanted him to have the operation and just get rid of the thing. On the other hand, I knew that there were risks to the operation. Well, of course there are risks to any operation. I had read about a prostatectomy on the internet and knew that the specific risks were impotence and incontinence.

Everything became more difficult. Mealtimes brought the need to talk about something when all that either of us could think about did not bear talking about any more. I sat toying with my green beans trying not to show Oliver what I felt because it had to be his decision entirely. It was his body. But it was my body too. Man and wife is one flesh says the Bible. What happened to him also happened to me in a sense. Perhaps Oliver knew that at some level but couldn't bear it. So he got very angry and impatient and when I asked what he thought would be best he yelled at me: "How the fuck do I know?" I found that hard to bear and melted away to my desk and looked at my e-mail through tears.

I thought of Margaret and how much I would like to be with her and have her silent, supportive self beside me or at least near me. I wondered how I would wait until I could see her. I remembered how it was at work when I had felt equally helpless. There was a financial crisis of government funding as usual in the prison service. I had not paid a great deal of attention to it so I was not prepared when one morning I opened a letter saying that the funding for the befriending service that my organisation was contracted to offer was to be cut by fifty per cent. I just sat and felt waves of heat over my whole body. How could we survive? How could we pay the salaries? The amount of work that could be done would be cut by at least half. Could we even do that? You can't just cut and hope that what you have left will work in the same way. Take away some of the activity and the rest of the activity is bound to suffer. Immediately, in that first morning, I was turning over plans for ways of making up the income so that staff could be paid to work in the prisons and in the training department. The need of the prisoners hadn't gone away even though the support for the work might have done.

I found that I was not angry at that point but I became immensely frustrated when I immediately tried to ring the bureaucrat who had written the letter. I knew one person in the ministry's finance department but was told that she was on annual leave for the next three weeks. When I told the deputy what I wanted to talk about, he said that I could talk to him of course but he would not be able to do anything about it. The directive had come down from on high, he said. Then in a hollow voice he added "Home Office" as though that explained everything. I put the phone down and sat back in my chair staring at the ceiling. After some time a thought emerged: I should ring Barbara as she is now the Chair of BOT and tell her about what has happened. But instead I summoned the Management Group.

"We have a problem," I told them, "but we can solve it. We need to diversify. We need to develop new funding streams. Let's get our ideas together."

"Have you told Barbara?" asked Anita.

"Not yet. Let's get some ideas together first and then we can present a plan, not just a disaster. I want to know what we can market and how we could get other contracts. Let's see what ideas we can get immediately and then we will meet again tomorrow and see what we can all dream about tonight." That last bit was partly a joke but also I hoped that someone would have some useful ideas and I was quite prepared for them to come from dreams.

I could see that they were worried and thought I should probably tell Barbara straight away but I was determined to wait until I had something positive to add. The funding cut was not my fault but I felt responsible for it. I would be the messenger and I felt that I might be shot.

The Management Group came up with several ideas. They sat with calculators and managed to make up the lost sum with potential sales of space on the website, marketing consultancy offering management training and lastly, my own big idea: get the churches to support what they were doing. "Not just the churches but the synagogues, the mosques, the temples, everyone," I said, with as much enthusiasm as I could. "They all believe in supporting the most vulnerable and there will be members of all their congregations in prisons and doing prison visiting."

Julie was the new Head of Training Services who had just been appointed. She was looking very unhappy. "I don't see how we can promise any of this. It's all just a hope. You need something more definite." I swallowed my first response—it was too angry. I was particularly angry because Julie said *you*, not *we*. What I said was still angry, but not as enraged as I felt. "'Yes of course that's what we want but how would you think we could achieve that?' We have to be hopeful at this stage. We can't promise anything can we?" Julie pursed her lips and kept quiet. I knew that I had been unfairly vehement to her but I was still angry enough myself to want to leave Julie to her own anger. I did not think that Julie would do any harm because after all, I had appointed her and entrusted a good deal of work to her.

Mike, who was Anita's deputy and came from Ghana, was enthusiastic. His father was a Protestant but his mother was Jewish and he often spoke up for the Jewish or African perspective: "The Jewish communities will want to get involved. But you will need to watch some of the others who will want to proselytise. You know that there is a recruiting drive for fundamentalists in the prisons. We are already worried about that and if we get funding from one group, it could be used to persuade the others to help us but you will have the danger of the quid pro quo. That is," he added kindly, "they may want to persuade our staff to allow them a bit more space to put their views across."

I heard him and could see that he was right but I could not afford to let it stop me or even slow me down. This was an idea that in principle could bring in money: as much or more than was needed.

I drew up a rough and ready spread-sheet which showed that they could make up the lost income by the combination of new methods that had been discussed. I finally went home at about 11 p.m. with all the people on the bus, who had been to see films or had had some other kind of good time, and I felt some resentment for my lack of enjoyment. I spent the night mostly lying awake and seeing the figures in my brief, troubled dreams. I got up the next morning, with the feeling of distance of the very tired, uncomfortably aware that what I saw in my mind was just that: my own dream. I pushed that thought back down out of sight and as soon as I arrived in my office I rang Barbara and asked to meet her later that morning. At a coffee shop near Barbara's office we sat down divided by a latte and a cappuccino. I plunged straight in and told her that they had been let down by the Prison Service but that I had plans. Barbara was obviously very shocked. "Can you really do this?" she asked, "because if you can't, you will have to make staff redundant."

"We can do it' was all I said, but I heard myself committing the others as well, not just myself. "I'll let the Finance Group know that you have a possible solution here," Barbara said at last "and we will call an extraordinary meeting for Friday."

Against all reason, I was greatly relieved as I made my way back through the long streets of suburban Bradford to the office. I should have been much more anxious. When I sank into my chair I could no longer put off thinking about how to put all these promises into practice.

The first obvious problem would evidently be Julie. She wasn't at all caught up in enthusiasm and she would not put her heart into something that already made her cynical. I needed the team to be entirely enthusiastic. I needed them to believe that they could succeed because I knew how doubtful the whole enterprise really was. I decided that I must tackle Julie but I did not expect a great deal of resistance. I asked Julie to come and see me, but, aware that I could not give the reassurance that was needed, I sat awkwardly watching Julie pulling on one strand of her shoulder length hair. She was young and attractive but I had hoped that she was serious enough about what she did to become devoted to their work. She fiddled with the ends of her long blond hair but wouldn't look at up. "You seem unhappy," I offered.

"Well it isn't a very happy situation is it?"

"No" I agreed, "so that is why I want us to be proactive so that we can use the opportunity to make the organisation more self-reliant."

"You haven't got the right staff to do it, though. You need someone with real business experience because you are talking about increasing the business part of what we do. That's not something I'm good at. I'm a teacher not a business man or woman for that matter. Why don't you get someone in who really knows how to do it?" She had a point. I told her so and said I wanted to think about how we could bring in more of this sort of expertise.

I went home and thought long and hard. Clearly without money I could not create a new senior post. I might scrape together enough money to buy in consultancy but that would probably cost just as much and would not last long. In the middle of the night I woke up with the solution. I would offer to work fewer hours and would appoint a part time business manager with the salary that I was giving up. If he or she was successful, the salary for a future post would be brought in. If not, the job would be abolished before one year. I would show the staff that I was willing to put myself on the line for the good of the organisation. I went back to sleep and slept better than I had for many nights.

At its meeting on Friday, I presented my idea to the Finance Group. They were not enthusiastic. Barbara said she would have to consult the rest of the Trustees before accepting such an offer and changing the role of the Chief Executive. I was incredulous and dismayed. I had not expected gratitude exactly but it had never occurred to me that they would not accept my offer. In fact I had not thought of it as an offer. I had assumed that I would just do it as an executive action and that it was not a matter of governance for the Trustees.

A week of misery and uncertainty passed. At last I received a letter from Barbara saying that the Trustees had considered my "suggestion" at their dinner at Lady Young-Talbot's house. They had decided that they could not allow me to do as I had suggested. The post of Chief Executive must be full time. They made no comment on the plan that I had offered to deal with the future funding of the post. They also ignored my point that with the financial stringency at the time, there would be able executives being made redundant and therefore available to us for the sort of salary that could be offered. They just simply said no.

I continued to be amazed. What was the matter with them? I had mentioned to the Management Group that more expertise was needed and they had heard the proposal to the Finance Group. Now I just had to tell them that, with no reasons given, the plan had been thrown out. I was furious and my pride was deeply hurt. I told them with what was probably barely concealed irony that no doubt the Trustees had their reasons but I was not sure what they were. In any case, they were to manage with the people that they had. "Why," asked Julie, "do we not get someone on the BOT with that sort of expertise?" I was tempted to tell her that they thought they already had that sort of expertise. In fact, I kept my mouth shut and looked round. Have we got any ideas about who might be helpful? "Well," Anita, said, I remember that Gerald, who was the Director before Oswald, was very good at bringing in funding. Maybe he would be willing to come and bring in some of the people he knows. He is still very supportive of the organisation. I beamed at her. "That is an excellent idea. Will you ask him if he's willing in principle? I will mention it to Barbara." She agreed and again I was able to feel that they had come to a useful conclusion including Julie more than before.

I suddenly thought that I felt a satisfaction similar to my feeling when my two older children included the younger ones in a plan or a discussion. I I felt a great relief because I knew that I had hardly ever included my little sister in my plans or my games. I suppose I thought that now I could repair something in a way even thought my sister was left with her experience and all that meant to her. My parents had made me feel vaguely guilty but because they would not know the extent of my meanness, they were not able to tell me how difficult and unpleasant I was when I had a friend to play and would play at teasing her and making sure that we climbed trees that she couldn't reach and hid in places where she wouldn't find us. Now I have some inkling of what it is like to be left out from the BOT and I know how much it hurts. With Julie, I am not sure whether it was Julie leaving me out or Julie excluding herself that I minded the most.

The next morning I managed to lift the phone and speak to Barbara. I was able to be positive and polite again because I felt that I could see the glimmer of hope for the future. "The Management Group has a proposal to make," I began. 'We thought that as you do not want us to appoint a business manager, we could strengthen the business input in BOT. Anita is sounding out Gerald to see whether he would be willing to become a trustee and bring in his contacts to tell us how to succeed with our new enterprises. There was silence at the other end of the line. "I'll see what they think. Lady Young-Talbot is giving us a great deal of help and will supply what we need, I think."

"Oh," I said, "good. Is she going to pass it on to me?"

"She thinks you should have a fund raiser and will pass it on to him."

"So it's not my job?"

"It's your job to appoint a fund raiser and manage him."

Once again, I was blocked and frustrated. The good thing was that at last I had something positive to tell the staff even though no-one appeared to have thought how to pay a fund raiser. At least it would take some of the weight off my shoulders. I set about the process of hiring Lana.

Margaret had said nothing for some time. Alice just carried on talking but when she mentioned the weight on her shoulders, she suddenly thought of payment. She had been talking about money and her worries about it and had been coming for about five weeks and there had been no mention of paying. "Don't you want me to pay you?" Alice said suddenly after a short pause. Margaret looked at her. "Of course I want you to pay me. You know what you owe me, I think."

Alice felt deeply shamed. Of course she knew exactly what she owed and she realised that she had just been waiting to be asked for it. Why had she waited? Then it occurred to her: she would have been able to feel that she was doing something for Margaret and if she asked her for the money, it would show her that that she wanted it. But Margaret didn't ask her for it, which meant she was invited to offer it to her. Who owed what to whom? Alice felt it was all a muddle and was furious again. "Why didn't you give me a bill like any normal person? I would have paid you. You know I would." She tried to hold back the tears but found herself crying. Once again she felt misjudged and undervalued. This was exactly what happened with the Trustees. They made her feel useless. Now Margaret, whom Alice valued so much, was doing the same. She went home and howled into her pillow for an hour until Oliver came home and she pulled herself together.

At the next session Alice walked in and silently handed a cheque to Margaret for all that she owed. She was still both angry and humiliated although not quite sure why she felt so ashamed. Perhaps Margaret had seen some greed in her, some unwillingness to part from the money. That possibility made her deeply ashamed. She knew that she was not paying enough anyway and Margaret was letting her get away with it. "You were expected to take the responsibility for the money without the help and support of the Trustees," was all Margaret said. Alice was surprised that she would say so much. But she felt better because she understood that perhaps Margaret could see that she needed more help and support. "So I decide when to pay you?" Alice asked abruptly.

"I think you might pay me at the end of every month."

"I don't want to have to pay you at all," Alice muttered. Then it dawned on her. Of course, she hadn't paid because she couldn't bear the idea of paying her at all. She just wanted Margaret to want to see her. How would she ever know about that if she was paying to be seen? Then it came to her. Margaret was seeing her for less than the standard because she *did* want to see her. That thought was pure joy. Of course she said to herself, "don't be silly," but she could not drop the idea once she had thought it. It brought immense peace and happiness and she

was able to go home and listen to Oliver telling her about his decision
to accept the brachytherapy.

I told him that I would support him in every way while he had
the procedure. The consultant had looked at his MRI scan and
had decided that the tumour was clear and sufficiently localised
to be treatable in this way. "It's good news'," he said. This is less
risky than the operation and it has good results so far. Mr Roberts
says he has carried out these treatments and is very pleased with
the results so far. I have to go in over two nights and then rest for
two more days. Then I can go back to work.' I hugged him and
said that I was sure he would be all right and I would be with him
every step of the way. Then I lay awake all night wondering what
exactly it meant. Would it just stop the tumour from growing or
would it make it shrink? "Don't be silly," I told myself. It can only
stop it from growing. Maybe it's so small that he can live with it.
One clearly good thing, I realised in the night, was that this would
be done by the NHS. I would not have to find the money myself.
Here again, I was not being asked to pay now. Pay later? I asked
myself. I suppose I must.

I woke up feeling sad but told myself just to get up and get on
with something and not dwell on the down side of what might
go wrong. I was only too well aware that things might go wrong.
Oliver was in the bathroom. He seemed to spend more time in there
than he had before. Or perhaps I was just imagining that. I told
myself to concentrate on the positive but could not control the
thoughts which circled back to the risks. I realised that one of the
main problems for me was that I did not know what the risks were
and felt that I couldn't ask Oliver. He was talking a little and if
I took too much advantage of that he would get into a rage and not
talk any more at all. That had happened so much in the past that
I had learned not to test the limits of his tolerance.

Testing the limits of tolerance began to be the main concern at
work. On the morning when I had just come to the conclusion that I
would make an announcement, the telephone rang. It was Barbara
and her voice immediately let me know that something was seriously wrong. "I'm sorry to have to tell you that one of the Trustees
has a serious problem." She stopped, apparently debating how to
put something. I waited in much the way that I had experienced

Margaret waiting. "It's Jacob," she said at last. "He went back to the Congo for a holiday and he has been interned. Or at least we think he has. As you know, he is a member of the BOT Finance Group and he had access to all the bank accounts. He has sent an e-mail to Arthur saying that he is in trouble and he has had to borrow some money to get out of prison and to get back to the UK. A large amount of money has disappeared from the account and we don't yet know how the two things are related or whether they are related." I could not believe my ears. "But he couldn't have withdrawn any money. You need two signatories for any action at all."

"Yes, that is true but he knew the signatures well."

I realised that Barbara was saying that he might have forged the other signature. I thought of Jacob, small and quiet and always courteous and helpful. "But he would never do such a thing. He must be really in trouble. We will have to try to help him. How can we find out?"

"That is just the problem. We do not know how we can find out and Arthur thinks that the only thing we could do, would be to send someone out there to see what is going on and help him if necessary. Of course the organisation will have to support whoever we decide to send if we do want to do that."

"So what have you heard? Have you heard from Jacob himself?"

"Arthur has an e-mail from him about the problem just before it appears to have happened. He was using his customary e-mail address and so Arthur is convinced that Jacob really is in trouble."

I had two conflicting sets of feelings. On the one hand, all this commotion would distract attention from the funding problem. What was it that Tony Blair was supposed to have done—burying bad news in some way. Well this might be a way of burying bad news. Secondly, I recognised that this might be an additional problem of huge proportions. Surely it was a scam of the sort that people received every day by e-mail. But what if it were not? What if something terrible had happened to Jacob and he had been so desperate that he had taken the money. No-one was going to reimburse a charity for what one of its own Trustees had done. What would happen if the money were really to have disappeared into some criminal gang? I hardly dared ask the next question. "How much did he take?" And after a pause: "If he took anything that is."

Barbara seemed to recollect herself. "We don't know yet that he took anything. Of course you will not tell anyone about this. It is not appropriate to discuss this now. Arthur will get in touch with your Finance Officer and we shall then talk further."

Our Finance Officer was a small muscular Yorkshire man, Peter Jamieson. He was a man of few words but he was a good account-ant. He would certainly be aware of it if a large amount of money had been drawn from one of the accounts. I asked him to come and talk to me immediately. He arrived with the minimum delay and sat expectantly. I found myself a little unsure. What was I allowed to say? Was I supposed to wait until Barbara had spoken to Arthur who would then speak to Peter. Maybe I should have waited. "I was wondering whether you have checked the amount in our accounts recently?" I asked. Peter looked at me in surprise. "Of course, we do reconciliation of the account that we are using every day. As you know we get a statement on our investments every month so I have not asked for that for three weeks but I will be getting it next week. Is there something you want to know in particular?" There was just a hint of irritation in his voice. He was evidently wonder-ing why he had been removed from his comfortable corner with his computer and his assistant, Otto, poring over the spread sheets that they both loved. "There may be a problem," I said, "but I think Arthur is going to get in touch with you. You'd better get back to your phone and come and see me again after you have spoken to him." "Very well" said Peter without more ado and made his way neatly out of the room.

I sat and again found myself reeling. How could this happen? There had been little enough money before and now apparently there was even less. At least there was no problem about whether or not or how to tell people. I was specifically forbidden to tell any-one. At first that was a relief but gradually, like a bit of grit in an oyster it irritated and grew bigger until it produced not a pearl but a carbuncle.

The next day Peter duly appeared outside the door looking mis-erable. I resignedly asked him to come in. "Tell me" I said.

"Well, you know," he began, "I think you already have an idea of what has gone on." I swallowed my pride. "Tell me" I said again.

Peter hunched his shoulders as if to ward off a blow and said very fast: "We are not sure what has happened but we are missing

£100,000 from the current account. Arthur seems to have some idea. It must have happened yesterday. How could it happen? What can we do? I'm sure it can't have been anything to do with Otto. He's very upset because he thinks we will blame him."

I recognised the mixture of guilt and defiance. It was exactly what I felt about Jacob. Although I had no right to speak, I said "Don't worry Peter. I know it wasn't anything to do with you or Otto." Then I thought how stupid I was to say that. I did not know that it wasn't anything to do with them.

I was aware that I did not want it to be anything to do with them but I should keep my mouth shut until I did know more. I thought I would like to know what Arthur said but did not wish to show just how much I was kept in the dark. All I could do was promise Peter that I would have to discuss further action with the Trustees and would tell him as soon as I knew any more. Even that was a promise that I might not be able to keep but I made it anyway.

For half an hour I sat staring numbly at my computer screen. What else could go wrong? I felt paralysed and was not able to do much more than repeat over and over again to myself, "I must let people know." Just as I was reaching out my hand to the phone to summon the Management Group, it rang. Of course it was Barbara. "Obviously, the money has gone. You and Peter are the only ones who know about this terrible situation. You will not tell anyone else until we have decided how to proceed. I will tell you tomorrow morning how we intend to proceed."

"Have you told the police?"

"Not yet."

"I think you must do that immediately or we become accessories maybe."

"I appreciate that you have had a shock but when you are thinking clearly again you will realise that there is no need for you to tell us what you think we should do. This is a serious matter and we will tell you tomorrow what we expect from you. In the meantime I expect your loyalty to the organisation."

I spent a night frozen in a panic. I had no idea what the Trustees were going to decide or why. I knew that whatever they decided I would be expected to find the money to make up for the two gaps that had opened up. I thought that there might be a way of regaining the hundred thousand that seemed to have been stolen. Maybe the insurance covered theft or fraud. In fact it must. The problem would be bad enough if it were only the funding but what would the fallout be if there was general suspicion that one of the Trustees had stolen the money? How would the staff and the supporters deal with such a position?

The next morning, Barbara rang as she had promised although not until about 12 by which time I was almost ready to ring her in desperation. The conversation did not resolve very much. She said that not all the Trustees had been informed yet so nothing was to be said at all. They had not decided when or whether to inform the police. "Maybe we can deal with this very unpleasant matter ourselves." I was horrified at this idea but had no choice in the matter. Perhaps it would be all right since no-one seemed to know what kind of crime had been committed. "Maybe," I suggested to Barbara, "Jacob has just borrowed some money and will return it to us." "Maybe," agreed Barbara.

I could not contain my feelings. I decided that I could tell Oliver what was happening since he was not involved in any way. He was appalled. "There has been a major theft. At least it's major in your terms," he said. "You really should be reporting it. If you don't, your insurance will certainly not be sympathetic."

"Oh dear," I agreed. "That is just what I feared. We need any help we can get from insurance, so I will say that."

I recognised that I wanted help. Managing this whole mess on my own seemed too much. My urge to tell people about what was happening was part of my need to be supported. I had lost my confidence along with the money that had been taken away. I thought that I might feel better if I was able to make an announcement and bring everyone else into the problem area.

I wanted everyone to recognise that something important had happened and knew that I must either tell the staff about the problems and give them the idea that something could be done about it or not tell them and risk that they would in any case find out. The next Management Group was meeting to discuss the existing funding problem and agreed that I would speak to a staff meeting for the next week and let them know what was happening and at the same time announce the plans for making up the shortfall. I was so anxious about what I could and could not say that I found it difficult to speak clearly on anything. Julie appeared to be putting her energy into the plans that she had although she clearly thought that I was not doing a very good job with the Trustees. I was beginning to realise that my job entailed winning them over, not just complaining when they didn't seem to understand what I was saying to them.

Luckily a staff meeting was scheduled for the following week. They were held quite often to give people a chance to say whatever was on their minds. The result was often great explosions and expressions of anger which upset the non-professionals but which the managers took as useful and healthy. I felt that much as I disliked being attacked in those meetings, I preferred attacks to be out in the open and in a place where I had a chance to respond to what was being said. I knew that there would always be muttering in the staff common room. There always was but the fury that reached me in the meetings must have given vent to some of it and once heard, there was a chance to do something about the often quite small problems that were highlighted. I remembered arranging changes like putting "occupied" signs on doors so that people knew when they could knock and enter. This meeting would be more difficult. There was no immediate solution but the mostly part time staff would not be able to get to grips with the full meaning of it. At least so I thought.

I let Barbara know that I would tell the staff about the funding problem but not the theft at the next meeting. "I will come and help you" she announced. "Oh I don't think that will be necessary," I managed. "Yes. I think the Trustees should be represented when you talk about this critical situation." I shut my mouth and smouldered. The possibility that she might genuinely intend to be helpful disappeared out of the window like a wisp of smoke and I added the conversation to my already heavy load of anger and resentment against their behaviour but I said nothing. It never occurred to me that Barbara might have gathered and noted my reaction was even though I said nothing more. The meeting was absorbing all my attention. I spent a few wakeful hours going over possible words in the middle of the night until I thought that I had arrived at a way of putting the funding part of the problem in a benign and unfrightening way.

When the time of the meeting arrived, the usual group of about a dozen people turned up. Although there were about a hundred people on the books, many did not live in Bradford and I had not expected many. They all had jobs in other places, at least part time, and could not really be expected to turn up in the day time when they were not normally working for us. I would write up the notes and circulate them in e-mails which a few people might read. Julie however was horrified: "Why don't we require them to come to at least a minimum number during the year?" she demanded. As usual I said that she could see her point and that maybe we would do that in future. It seemed the least of my problems. At that time I was focussing entirely on the meeting that we would have on the next day.

An hour before the meeting Barbara had arrived. "I have something very unfortunate to tell you. Jacob has been in touch with Arthur and has let us know that he has no possibility of returning the money and will not be returning to the UK. We do not know what happened except that this is very unusual behaviour. We have decided that it is better for the organisation not to broadcast this even though we think it might not be his fault. It looks bad and we are asking you to keep quiet for now."

"But what about the Charity Commission? What about the accountants? You can't just lose £100,000 without anyone noticing."

"You will let the BOT worry about that. You will concentrate on fundraising. You can just tell the managers that the BOT is aware of the loss and will decide what to do." I was furious but I summoned the Management Group: "Apparently a large sum is missing. Peter knows about it and we are to leave it to the BOT to decide what to do." Peter was angry too and said without hesitation "Yes, £100,000 is a large sum." There was a stunned silence. Julie reacted first. "We must find out what has happened so that we can prevent any further losses. How can someone take so much from us? You must investigate it immediately Peter."

"I can't do anything. I have been told not to mention it." There was silence again. "It's time for the Staff Meeting. We'll discuss this later." Burning with shame at my helplessness I stormed out of the office and into the meeting scheduled for 5.30. As usual, about twelve people had turned up, and were eating crisps and drinking whatever Desmond, the HR assistant had provided. Although the Hall would have held about a hundred, I was not displeased with the turnout because it was what I had expected. Barbara, however, was not impressed. "Where are they all?" she asked loudly when she entered the room. I ignored her and began to welcome those who were there. "Just a minute" said Barbara, "I would like to know where all your colleagues are." I tried to pull myself together and said to the assembled group that I was delighted to welcome Barbara since many of the staff would not know who she was. They were all looking at each other in a somewhat puzzled way with brows furrowed. "Was this a real question from Barbara or not?" "Yes," she said, "you might well look unhappy. This is a disgrace. There are at least a hundred people on the staff and you should make sure that your colleagues are here. I'm sorry but this will just not do. I shall be writing to you all about it."

I felt a sense of unreality. No-one had ever tried to take over a meeting in this way before. I felt even angrier because I knew that I had not tried to get more people to come to the meetings. At the same time, I did not think it was Barbara's job or that she had any right to speak to the staff as she did.

Perhaps that was the last straw. Whatever the cause I went far beyond what I had intended. I told the staff about the funding problem in the way that I had planned and then I added: "We also have another serious problem in that a sum of money has disappeared from our bank account." "£100,000" said Peter. "The BOT is looking into it and will no doubt let us have the results of their investigation in due course." One glance at Barbara's face was enough to show me that this had been a crazy thing to say. Barbara got up and left. The staff buzzed. "Well, I will just give you a few ideas about what we plan to do to make up the shortfall and no doubt the BOT will support all our efforts." I told the meeting what I planned and the staff left in puzzled, horrified silence.

In the bus on the way home I saw an old woman helping a child to hold on to her as the bus hurtled jerkily through the traffic. Sometimes people's motives are good. Slowly I began to face the reality that I had gone too far. I should have waited and let the BOT stay in charge. Now I too was part of the problem, not just an innocent bystander. The thief as I must now think of Jacob, had taken away more than just the money. He had stolen my self-respect.

CHAPTER FIVE

Circumvented

A lice told Margaret that she was afraid that she was feeling increasingly paranoid. At the very least she was lonely. The Trustees were not with her at all on any of this. "Have they had the chance to be?" asked Margaret. Alice dismissed this. "They could be supportive at any time." But as usual she found that Margaret's comment was a germ that grew, multiplied in her head and could not be ignored. She had not given them a chance. She had enjoyed growing more and more bitter and resentful and there was no response from Barbara to make her feel otherwise. In fact, she gave ample opportunity for escalating feelings of powerlessness every time they spoke.

I appointed Lana as the new Fund raiser but then Barbara told me that I should fire her. I declined to do that and that hastened my own downfall. I hesitated, wanting to give Lana another chance. I wanted her to succeed and somehow I thought that Lana must know what to do. "If only I could give her a bit more time," I thought, "all would be well." I brooded over the actions of the Trustees and in my imagination wrote many letters to them with innumerable ways of showing how angry I was and how they had made my job impossible. I was by no means reluctant to concentrate on this grievance because thinking about Oliver and possible loss of him was too painful.

Defiantly I spent time helping Lana to set up a fund raising event. It was to be an evening with a celebrity, inviting donors to come and meet a well-known person. Lana was against the whole thing but was not proposing an alternative with any kind of rapid result so grudgingly she agreed to try to find a celebrity. Eventually she came up with the local MP. He was not enthusiastic for work with prisoners. In fact, he seemed to be of the "why don't you just train them for a job?" school of thought. Very few of the donors from the constituency seemed enthusiastic about meeting him and those from further afield had not even heard of him. When the evening came, many of our staff were there out of loyalty but only a handful of potential supporters came and not enough tickets were sold to pay for the wine that was bought. It was a failure.

I had put a great deal of time into this event which all seemed to be wasted. In particular I needed to work on my new plan to win the co-operation of the Churches. I needed Gerald who had already made good contact with some Roman Catholics, Methodists and Anglicans but not with many from other faiths. I did not think he had talked much to the more evangelical churches but at least he could have helped with a good start. But I had to tell him that the Trustees did not want him after all. I was struggling with the uncomfortable thought that it might have been my fault for mentioning the possibility to him before I had their agreement, but it had never occurred to me that they would not seize on it. I still had no idea what their problem was, other than that I had suggested him.

It was at the time of doubt just beginning to show that downfall opened up like the jaws of hell smiling and beckoning. Ironically, it was an old colleague of Anita who sealed my fate. She was called Susan and she had been on the staff a few years before until she retired. She came to have lunch with Anita and they both came into the office after to talk about the problems. Anita told me about not being allowed to appoint a business manager and not knowing why. Susan snorted in scorn. "It's so obvious that it would help and they are saying no? You will have to tell them not to be so stupid!"

"No," I told her, "I can't tell them that. In fact I just have to accept whatever they say and whatever they do. They are my bosses collectively, through Barbara of course."

Susan looked at me as though she could not believe that anyone could be so pathetic. "Well, I'll write to them then. I will write to them and get a group of us together to tell them what we think."

"No, no," I panicked "don't do that. You'll get me fired and you and anyone else into terrible trouble."

Susan thought for a minute, frowning. "Well, don't you bother about it. I'll think of something and I won't involve you. But I am going to do something I can tell you. They deserve to get a whole lot of stuff poured over their heads and I'm the one to do it. Because I am an ex-employee I can get some people together and we can let them know somehow that they are being absolutely stupid."

I stopped thinking and simply said, "Well I don't want to know anything about it," but I felt a kind of shameful pleasure. I wanted the Trustees to be told that they were idiots and the sooner and the more vociferously they were told the better. I managed not to think about the repercussions much after that first warning. I was totally seduced by the idea that Susan and whoever she recruited would not involve me. I told myself that I was really happy with that and decided that they could manage their own affairs. In fact, when I came to think about it, as long as they weren't current staff, they couldn't be touched. "Well, don't include current staff," was all I said.

At the time, Alice found that she was able to feel ruthless. She was not paying as much attention to the dangers at work as she later understood had been needed. Oliver was beginning his treatment. She watched him. That was the hardest thing. She could do nothing but watch. If only she could have done something she might have felt better but all she could do was watch as he went for his injections. She told Margaret that there had been one moment of intimacy when he told her at lunchtime that he had slept badly because of a dream. He had dreamt of rats gnawing at him and how frightening that was. She wasn't sure whether to press him to tell her more but she just waited. He didn't say anything but he was clearly disturbed by his own mind. Later that afternoon she decided to say something more. "Maybe you were bothered by the treatment, and thought of yourself being eaten up?" she tried. He looked at her and for a moment she glimpsed the misery that was not far beneath the surface. "Maybe" he said and retreated into his room. She thought he cried but he would not have wanted her to see, much less talk to him.

Alice had to accept that she knew about this and his face stayed in her mind even though he took care to keep out of her way. She had to keep on working and if she shut herself in with what she was doing with a firm grip on her thoughts she could sometimes manage to forget him for a while. And for a while nothing else happened.

Then came the day when she received a message from Barbara to ring her as soon as possible. Alice rang her within half an hour. Her voice was thin and stretched as she announced that something very serious had happened. She had received a letter that said it had come from some of the staff. Alice was to find out who had sent it and make sure that they were punished appropriately. She rang off. Alice sat while waves of anxiety washed over her. To her horror, she began to understand that she felt sorry for Barbara. Her thoughts became more of a battle ground when she described them to Margaret: She began to realise that the question of what to do about Jacob was taking its toll of her energy as well. As far as the letter was concerned, Alice didn't know for certain but she did have a pretty good idea about what had happened and who had done it. But done what? She had no idea what they might have said but she did know who had probably organised the letter. How could she have been so foolish as to let it happen? And yet, could she have stopped it? How could she have been so heartless as well as foolish? The thoughts went round and round the same tread-mill. She recognised a small sliver of pleasure mixed with the anxiety and the guilt. Perhaps they now could see that what they were doing was wrong.

> The Trustees were making my life impossible. I was angry, angry and Susan's letter apparently had done just exactly what I wanted it to do. I couldn't want it to be otherwise. And yet, I was being told that I must find the culprits and make sure that they were punished "appropriately." I sat in my office chair, paralysed. What could I possibly do? Should I tell the Managers what had happened? Barbara had said that the whole matter should be treated with the utmost seriousness. What on earth could they have said that had made such a stir among the Trustees? I wondered and worried. Any pleasure I might have felt at first faded fast. This was a bad thing to have happened. I decided to tell the Management Group about this latest problem. Then Barbara rang back. "What have you decided to do?" she snapped. "Well," I said slowly, "it's

difficult to know where to begin since I have so little information. What did the letter say?"

"I can't tell you that without authorisation from the whole BOT. You must simply find who wrote it and make them aware that this is a serious disciplinary offence. They should lose their jobs."

At this I lost my sympathy and let my anger get the better of me in a counter-productive and damaging way. "I really think we need to know what this is all about before we can even begin to think whether punishment is appropriate at all, never mind what it should be."

I tried to keep my voice even and objective but knew that my own feelings must be audible. Barbara heard the anger and responded to it. "You will do what I tell you or you also will be disciplined." I paused, horrified. How could they have reached such a stage of open hostility? I back- tracked at once. "Of course, I will do what you say. I just think it would help me if I had more detail."

"Maybe later," she said. "For now you will work with what I have told you." She rang off. I realised that the anxiety about the money was all being channelled into the new question that was being left unanswered.

For the second time, I was faced with telling staff that I had not been told the reasons for the actions of the Trustees. They did not trust me and I was now furious with them. I told the Management Group that the Trustees had received a critical letter and that it purported to come from staff. They immediately wanted to know what it was about. I had to tell them that I had no idea. Again I felt that I was humiliated and had lost all desire to make it look as though everything was all right. Humiliation took over from sympathy and swamped the small tender shoots of remorse. I said that I thought that it must be someone who was opposed to current actions but I could not imagine why that might be. Anita looked at me quizzically as though she was well aware of my anger but had decided that it would not help anything for her to say so. "But our staff would not do anything without telling us," said Julie in genuine amazement. "They are very outspoken. You know what my meetings can be like. They say the most outrageous things at times but they do say them; they don't just skulk in corners. Why on earth would they want to write to the Trustees? It doesn't make any sense." The others all agreed. It did not make sense that staff should have written it and I knew or thought I knew that they had not.

The Management Group began to talk about what they should do. Everyone had a different view about how much should be said and to whom they should say it. My turbulent feelings led me to want to say as little as possible but I could see that the others were full of righteous indignation and did not want to let the matter rest. "We should tell everyone, get rid of the secrecy and the bad feeling that it causes," said Anita with her usual wisdom. In the end they reached a compromise and decided to tell only the most responsible staff and not spread anxiety and disaffection round the whole organisation. Julie said she wanted to speak to her staff and she would do it in her own way.

I was intrigued and appalled at the uproar that the letter had caused. I wondered whether to ask Susan what the letter had said but decided not to get any further involved. Something had been born and would now grow into whatever shape it must. I thought of the rats gnawing at poor Oliver's body and wept. I thought of the gift that Susan had intended to give. I had certainly thought of it as a gift.

Alice confessed to Margaret that she had been pleased to receive this gift and to feel empowered and transformed by it. Now she could see that this gift had become the most deadly of debts. She had not fully appreciated how much she would have to pay.

Barbara began to ring at regular intervals, about two hours apart to ask what I had done since the last time. I began to experience her as the tyrant whose presence caused all my problems. She began to diversify her phone calls a little, asking whether I had now fired Lana as instructed. I stayed doggedly polite but unresponsive but knew that I was making Barbara angrier too. I did not take that as any kind of warning. Because I now felt some sympathy for Barbara and the others I felt that I was no longer responsible. In fact I felt powerful because I could give or refuse what Barbara wanted. For once I felt that I had the upper hand. I had a headache that gnawed at me but I was able to ignore it and carry on with my work. I was deciding the rules of the game in my own mind.

When Alice told Margaret what this was like, Margaret looked concerned. "Maybe this is what it would have felt like to get your own back on the bullies at school?"

Alice put her hand to her head. "You might be right. This time I am not the poor one without the right games kit. I am the one who holds some of the cards even though the cards that I hold are just knowledge, not the kind of wealth that interests young girls."

"Is this making you ill?" Margaret asked after a pause.

"I've just got a headache. It's nothing. I'm a bit stressed at the moment. I'll be fine when this trouble at work settles down."

After two more days of stalemate something did happen. The first I knew of it was that Anita came into her room looking pale and anxious. "I have something to tell you" she began. "Sit down. Whatever is the matter?" I asked her. "It's Joanna, Susan's friend who lives in York. Apparently she has told Julie that she knows who wrote the letter. It is a group of Susan's friends who are all people who have gone through our training programmes and some of them used to work for us, although they don't any more. She says she's unhappy that other people are getting blamed and she's going to tell Barbara. Apparently Joanna was very keen to take the blame and there does seem to be a lot of that. She says you taught her once and she thought that she owed it to you to send the letter but now it's all gone wrong. So I don't know what we can do but it's a bit of a mess isn't it?"

I felt the same. It was a mess. The whole thing had developed into a school story of the sort that I used to read avidly when I was about fourteen. I remembered the tone of unhealthy but intense excitement: "I will tell Miss Plunkett that you were the one who left the window of the dorm open and then you will be expelled." I had loved the plots and the characters then. I did not love them now they had become real. I was aware of a sort of tension in myself that would be relieved only by action and, even though that action might not be good for anyone, I would rush on with it. I knew that I was in a dangerous state and remembered that Margaret said "You are risking a lot" and yet I could not turn away from revenge and all that it seemed to offer. In that overheated state I rang Barbara. "I know something about the letter" I said without preliminary "but I won't be able to do anything to punish the person or people concerned. Just tell me what it's about and I will get it all settled."

"You'll do nothing of the sort," said Barbara. "I require you to report back to me about what you have discovered but further than that is not your affair. We will decide who is to be punished and how. Now tell me what it is that you have discovered." I was thrown immediately into the paralysis that might have been expected. I had wanted to tell her something that would show that I was in control. I now understood that I would not tell her anything. What I said was an achievement in its minimalism: "I just wanted you to know that I am making progress and I will tell you as soon as I know anything."

"That is very disappointing," Barbara commented and hung up. I was left to stare at the painting of the sea on the wall behind my desk and to tell myself over and over again how stupid I was to have rung her.

This time, the Trustees did not leave it alone. Whatever the message had said had obviously hurt them a great deal, because the next thing I heard was that they wanted to meet with me on my own to discuss the "current serious state of your insubordination." I was not as worried about that message as I should have been. I did think that the use of the word "insubordination" was worrying, although it seemed to be understandable. I had after all refused to tell Barbara what she wanted to hear.

The meeting was shocking. It was at the luxurious city office of one of the Trustees who worked in the centre of Bradford. Each place at the big table was automatically set with a notebook and pencil and there was coffee and biscuits on the sideboard. They were all there when I arrived, having evidently had lunch, and they stared over my head in silence. Barbara began. "We won't keep you long. We just wanted to tell you the contents of this letter. Would you like me to read it to you or will you take it away and read it in your own time?" Curiosity overcame caution. "Oh, read it to me" I said and waited. "Very well", she said, "if that is your choice." She then proceeded to read the most unpleasant and difficult thing I ever remembered hearing:

"Since you have chosen to refuse to comply with the requirements of the Board of Trustees, we have no choice but to set you some targets which you must fulfil or face losing your position. We must emphasise that this is your last chance."

They said more besides but I could no longer hear. I left the building in the centre of a sort of emotional storm. I sat on a bench at the bus stop on the way home and tears blinded me. There were not many people around so it did not matter too much. In any case I could not help myself. I thought back over what I had done in order to feel less ashamed to tell Margaret what had happened: I had done my best for the organisation but had not had much time to show what I could do. My great mistake was not to have seen how much my independence would hurt and annoy the Trustees. Then I remembered the letter. That was what was making them so angry. I had not realised that whatever it said could have done so much harm. There was my pride too. I had wanted to be able to manage my own tasks and find solutions for the organisation's problems. That was not allowed. I should have run crying to Barbara and asked for help, not produced potential solutions. I had forgotten about their pride because I was too much taken up with soothing my own. With aching head and a sense of utter weariness I made my way back to the office instead of running home as I wished.

The next day I began to think about the tasks that had been set.

They were about the economics of the organisation. I had been given a target income to achieve for the current financial year which had five more months to run. Was it possible? Well it would have to be.

Never for one moment did I think that I might not take on the challenge. I didn't think of arguing about it either. One thing about which I was relieved was the privacy. The Trustees had shown enough consideration to tell me in private what they thought and had left it to me to decide what to say to anyone else. The rest of the afternoon was mercifully empty of appointments and I was able to sit and stare into the distance feeling angry and distressed but without any very positive plans. When I finally went home I walked past Anita's office and looked in. It was empty. A half formed idea became a compulsion. I wanted more than anything to tell her. I suppose that I wanted to talk to Margaret but it was all directed at Anita just then. I went back to my office and rang her at home, asking to go round to her house to talk something over. Anita agreed at once. Perhaps she could hear the pain in my voice.

Oliver was at home when I rang and told him I needed to stay late at a meeting. He wasn't pleased but he didn't argue. These days he was too distant to argue. I bought a bottle of wine and went straight to Anita's house which was in a quiet street in Leeds near the river. She lived with a friend called Dodie. I had met Dodie a few times because she sometimes came to look for Anita or to support the organisation when people were needed. They might have had a lesbian relationship but nobody commented on it and most people would just have thought it was not their business. My own feelings for Anita were complicated but I found that I didn't mind what Dodie's relationship with Anita might be. I was able to greet Dodie in a friendly way when she opened the door with a slightly apologetic grin. "Well hello" she said heartily, and I realised that she might mind me turning up like this. "I'm sorry to barge in" I said lamely "but I really need to talk to Anita." That seemed to help and I was ushered into a living room near the front door. "She'll be here in a minute. I think she's finishing seeing someone."

Anita came in as promised but while I was waiting I had to think properly about what I would in fact tell her.

Alice looked at Margaret at this point. She was simply watching and listening with attention as she always did. "It occurs to me," Alice said, "that it's odd to be telling you what I told someone else. It's kind of double layered. But it's all I can do, just give it to you second hand. And all you ever get is second hand. You get it from me and you don't know what's true and what isn't."

"Should I be worried about that?" Margaret asked.

"No course not" Alice snapped. "What would be the point of deceiving you? I might as well deceive myself." She said nothing and Alice knew she was going to have to think about all this again. She put it on one side for the moment. What came into her head then was the memory of just looking at Anita.

Anita was wearing one of her usual eccentric collection of skirts and scarves in a variety of colours from green and blue to scarlet. She was like a mediaeval stained glass window: clear and brilliant. I looked at her and found that I couldn't speak for the tears of anger and frustration that I was determined to hold back. She knew of course and she just stood up and put a hand on my shoulder. Gradually I got a grip on my feelings. "It's no good pretending to you," I said. "I am really unhappy. I want to tell you about it but I suppose I should keep it to myself."

"Here" Anita said, "we do things that we would not do at the office. Here I might hear things that I might not remember when we get back there." I understood and was profoundly thankful for her consideration. I trusted Anita entirely and if I held anything back it was not because I was afraid she would talk. "There are too many secrets. I would just like to tell you how I feel and then we will go back and behave properly. I think we can." She nodded. So I told her about the letter, at least as much as I knew and I confessed to wanting to punish the Trustees in some nebulous way. I told her that I was now being given an ultimatum and some targets, like an underperforming administrator. Anita stopped me there. "You find it humiliating to be given targets? Isn't that what our budget is every year?" I thought about that. "Yes it is and that is why additional targets now are really humiliating. Obviously I am working to fulfil that target and we all work our socks off to achieve it. Don't they trust us to be trying to do our best? Can't they see how hard we are all working?"

"It may be that they see that and it isn't what they are getting at." I waited. Anita didn't say any more, just looked at me.

"I realise that she does just what you do," Alice said to Margaret, "she gives me these enigmatic remarks and expects me to figure out what they mean."

"Well, you seem to like it when Anita does it." Alice thought about that. "I usually like it when you do it. It makes me think. And there is always more to do. I think that you will be here next time because you can't just leave me without explaining what you mean. So I need the demand and the need for an explanation because I am sure that you know that you're doing it. Anyway, Anita did it and I thought about what she had said."

"What were they getting at? Do you think they want me to bring in more money?" I asked Anita.

"Well of course they do. But don't you think they are after something else as well?"

Suddenly I saw something more. "They want me to be obedient don't they?"

"It looks as though that has become more important. Whatever the letter said, it seems to have to do with loyalty to you and therefore they are going to see that you don't owe everything to them. If you can function on your own and in your own right they won't like that. They want to bring you back to recognising that you are an employee. Can you accept that and behave accordingly?"

Anita was not asking only the question that seemed to be on the surface. I knew that I was an employee but I would not submit to the BOT. I thought that their actions recently had shown that they did not deserve respect. Anita knew that I was proud of my position as CEO. It had taken some courage to step up to it but now that I had done that I wanted to use the power that I had acquired for the good of the organisation. Anita could see that I would not easily submit to a group of people, some of whom at least I did not respect. Whether Anita respected them or not I did not know but I suspected that she might have agreed with me. It would not have helped either of us to discuss that aspect of what we both thought. "You're right," I said wearily. "I must stop defying them. That doesn't help." Anita tossed one of her scarves back over her shoulder and smiled. I knew that I had arrived at the right place but would I stay there? I didn't know but I thanked Anita and went home feeling much calmer and more confident.

Alice waited to see whether Margaret could accept that other people could be useful in this sort of role. "I get the feeling' Margaret said," that you want me to feel circumvented just the way you do with the Trustees. Alice was furious. It's nothing like that and nothing to do with it' she snapped. "I thought you would understand." "Let's not do that," said Margaret. Alice stopped in amazement. "You're not supposed to say things like that. I thought you were supposed to let me say whatever I want." Margaret said immediately, "I don't think we need to get into an argument about whether I understand you or not." Alice thought: "No. You're right. We don't. I know that you understand me better than anyone."

Alice went home feeling comforted.

The next day, Alice spoke to Barbara with every intention of being submissive and doing what she was told.

CHAPTER SIX

Be with me

Alice made her way into Margaret's room a month later with heavy steps. It had become the refuge that home had once been. She had longed for the moment when she would get there. She sat down and found she was too full of tears to speak. Margaret said nothing but waited attentively as always so that after a while Alice found that she could talk and she began:

> I went home and when I went through the front door there was that kind of silence that tells you that a house is empty. That's funny I thought. Oliver's car is outside; he must be here; where can he be? I went to check his study just as I normally do and there he was .... Sorry .... I managed to ring for an ambulance and the men were very kind. They were there in no time and they found me trying to do CPR. "It's all right" one of them said. "We'll take over now." They got him into the ambulance really quickly and we went to the hospital with blue lights and sirens and in a daze I followed his stretcher into the Accident and Emergency department. They told me to wait in a special room. I will never forget that room: the torn leather on some of the chairs, the horrible red plastic of the row of hard chairs against the wall. There was no window and that bothered me. How

would I know when the daylight came? I wanted to know what was happening but I dreaded being told. I don't know how long it was but it wasn't long. A young tired-looking doctor came and checked my name. Then he said "I'm sorry." He didn't need to say any more. I knew that Oliver was dead, probably before he left the house. Left the house. That sounds like a deliberate action doesn't it? I found that I felt sorry for the doctor. Poor kid. He didn't like the job of telling the poor wife, widow …. sorry …. He'll have to learn though. It goes with the job.

They were very kind. They left me with him for as long as I wanted and they told me what I needed to do.

"So now it's done," said Alice. "I have nothing else to lose. How will I live?"

Margaret spoke at last, clearly very moved and less able to be calm than usual. "You need time."

"Yes" Alice said, "they say time heals. Does it? I hope so. I feel as though I will never be healed". There was a long silence. "I have said that I will not go to work for two more weeks. But it's more than that. I will have to change this job. I need to stop enjoying resentment and being wounded and make it into something that is much less about loss and damage, them and us. I want this to be a job that doesn't cause me so much personal pain but gives me the chance to do as much as I can for it. Do you think that is right?"

Margaret recovered her usual careful position: "I can't advise you, you know but it sounds as though you feel that would be best at the moment."

"Yes. It's all I can do at the moment. I just want you to be with me. I'm not really asking you what you think. Just be with me."

"I'll be with you" Margaret said.

Alice went home feeling lighter. She still could not imagine how she would be able to live alone. She needed her children but did not want them to come home. She needed her friends but she did not want to talk to them, only to know that they existed. She had discovered what was important to her and it was not a job or a salary. It was Oliver who mattered. She could just reduce the impingement of the work environment to protect herself. After that she would not have to worry anymore and she would not make mistakes that would endanger others.

Worrying about money was something that she no longer did. She vaguely remembered how she had thought about the payment for

Oliver's treatment and she broke down thinking about how much she wished she had him back to worry about. But the reality was that she had no-one to worry about if she gave up worrying about her job. Her children would manage. Her parents would manage. She would manage.

I arranged a meeting with Barbara. This one was different. I told myself I would not cry. I decided that I would not mention Oliver, partly because I knew that I could not do so and stay controlled. I managed to say what I needed to without a tremor. "I have not been able to see things from your point of view. I have guessed what all this has done to you. All of us here need to say that we are grateful for what you are doing. I want to work with you now but I need more support. I need help to do this and I think you need my help."

Barbara was clearly astonished. "I can't understand this" was all she said.

"I'm not surprised that you don't understand. I only partly understand it myself. I just wanted to say that I want to change the relationship that we have to work with. It may be too late I don't know. But I will try if you will." I recognised that I was beginning to sound oppositional. I stopped. Barbara looked at me and seemed to see something of the iron determination that was enabling me to speak at all. She misinterpreted the source of the strength but decided to make the best of this new version of the difficult and hostile CEO.

"I will assume that you mean this for the best. I am sure that we will offer you any help that we can."

"Thank you" I said, although I was disappointed with this response. I was determined that I would not be pushed off course. Maybe Barbara was just not good at relationships and that meant that she needed help and a great deal of tolerance. "Could I have a meeting with Arthur to discuss the funding? The loss of the money that has been taken out of our account is another problem and I think I need to talk to him and maybe to Lady Young-Talbot as well. I wanted to discuss my ideas with them and get their advice. Do you mind if I arrange that?"

Barbara was again surprised. "Is that what you mean? That's fine. I thought you wanted us to raise the money."

I was amazed. I had never considered that the Trustees might be worried that I wanted to transfer responsibility to them. "I only wanted to be allowed to do what I thought would be helpful and manage matters with the staff that we have." We stared at each other in silence. Just a few sentences had changed the ground on which we stood. Neither of us had become any easier to work with and we both knew that new difficulties might be just beginning but we also now knew that we both wanted to make the best of what was possible. The prisons of Yorkshire would be better places for the new co-operation that might emerge.

I thought that my work would be different from now on and that was indeed the case but not in the way that I had expected. The Trustees had a meeting at Lady Young-Talbot's house and, out of that meeting, Barbara again asked to speak to me. "We have decided that we cannot continue as a Board. We think that this charity will have to close. It will have to close now before it incurs any debts. You have just enough money to make the current staff redundant. Our proposal to you is that you found a new charity. We have spoken to the Chief Inspector of Prisons and he is willing to support a charity that is set up with his aims in view. Three of us would be willing to form the nucleus of a new Board. I personally will not continue, nor will Lady Young-Talbot, but Arthur has agreed to be your first Chairman if you agree to do this."

I stared at her with a welter of mixed feelings. Gradually I began to distinguish the relief from all other feelings. I could begin afresh. I could begin with someone who would be supportive and would work with me. On the other hand, I would have an immense amount of work to found a whole new organisation. Could we stay where we were or would I have to find a new place? I could keep the staff that I wanted, perhaps, now including Lana. In any case, I could now choose. "Thank you Barbara" I said and I meant it.

Down the street towards the bus stop, fitful sunshine with just a hint of warmth in it greeted Alice. She was not far from crying for all that she had lost, yet here was perhaps a new beginning. She realised that she could not begin yet. First she would have to pay attention to the endings needed at work and in her own self to the loss of Oliver. But some day there would be something else. She arrived at the bus stop just as the bus drew up and she clambered onto it with gratitude.

PART II

WHAT MONEY MEANS

CHAPTER SEVEN

Money had to be invented

Money affects the life of most human beings, either by its presence or its absence. Money makes us both master and slave. Alla Sheptun captured this paradox: "Our power over money is real only inasmuch as we are able to understand its power over us" (Sheptun, 2011). Karl Marx located the whole of our ideological processes on an economic substructure (Brenner, 1986: 3), but even those ideologies that have no direct connection to Marxism are based on an understanding of economics and the effect of economic position on each of us as individuals and as the products of a society.

In the contemporary market, money is essential to enable exchange of goods. What is essential in the therapeutic encounter is exchange itself. Words are passed from one person to another and are received, held or rejected by each participant. The development of the process by which symbolic exchange becomes communication at all levels is one of the main subjects of this book. Indeed, in engaging with this book the reader might be receiving gifts from the writer but will not gain in the long run unless she is willing to bring her own ideas to assay the value of the currency being offered. Dipping into metaphor illustrates the way in which this chapter and this book makes and then uses its symbols. Its point is to ask the reader to consider the level at which money is important and yet to remember that it is only one strand of the complex of emotional and cognitive elements that operate in therapeutic encounters.

The origins of money

Money, the medium of commercial exchange in modern societies invites examination of the process by which we have come to use some objects to stand for others. Currency is a metaphor hat is recognised in each society. Money as the coinage of the market place has been with us a long time. Reiss-Schimmel (1993) summarises the possible sociological origins of money. Sacrifices to the gods were part of the religious culture for many societies. Reiss-Schimmel discusses the need for sacrifices as creating one of the earliest occasions when the value of an offering that would be appropriate to each level of society would be fixed by its priests. This would represent its value: "Le montant du sacrifice devint une valeur fixée." (1993, p. 31)—the total of each sacrifice became a fixed value. She suggests that in a given society, the priests were instrumental in setting value, in other words saying that one thing can represent another with equal value: "C'est ainsi que l'offrande, l'animal sacrificial, devint un moyen légal de payment." (Reiss-Schimmel, 1993, p. 33)—it is in this way that the offering, the animal sacrifice, became a legal medium of payment. A second point at which exchange was important was the arrangement of marriage. A woman or girl was given by her family to serve a man who would look after her and her children. The earliest need for exchange in primitive societies was related to blood and to marriage. In other words the first exchanges with prices and fixed values were about people and their gods, not commodities. Important life events brought the need for agreed means of exchange, value, and payment.

In spite of the level of obligation, even demand, that attended the payment of dowry and sacrifices to the gods, these were seen as gifts and formed part of what the French sociologist Mauss (1922) called the "gift economy." Gifts, he argued, were essential in forming social bonds because they created bonds of expectation. A gift implies an obligation, perhaps a need for repayment in some form. Certainly, the two forms of gifts mentioned above are both intended to bring some reward for the giver. Part of the nature of human society is that we spend time and energy in scrutinising gifts to decide what bonds and ties they bring with them.

As societies grew more complex, the possibilities for exchange increased. A farmer producing grain might want to exchange some of his produce for meat or fruit or skins which were not immediately available when he made his harvest. He needed a promise of future payment when the goods that he wanted were ready. The commodity exchanged was itself originally the only thing that changed hands. Barter economies might have developed with direct exchange of commodities, but valued items like cowrie shells came into use to convey the promise of payment in the future. Later the growing complexity of societies led to what is known as *fiat* money. Fiat is Latin for "Let it be" and conveys that money exists by decree and acquires its value from the authority who makes the decree. What is decreed is money that is purely symbolic and conveys value that is underwritten by an authority.

Fiat money in itself is nothing. The coins in themselves are worth something perhaps, but unless the coins are gold or silver they are not usually worth their face value—if the metal were worth more than the face value, it is likely that the coins would be melted down by scrap metal dealers. Metal, often gold or silver was by far the most useful means of symbolising value. It is portable, durable, and fungible. If a farmer wanted to exchange wheat for apples, something had to represent the wheat until the apples were ready to pick. In a small community you might trust your neighbours not to cheat you, but as soon as you go further afield the risk increases and you need more certainty. When you are dealing with strangers and expanding your trading options, a reliable, portable symbol of value is vitally important.

In the consulting room, the patient needs to be able to hold on to ideas that arise in the session and then to be able to use them later. In this sense the process begins with a trusted source that provides ideas that can be saved and used later.

Why use gold?

Freud used the metaphor of pure gold for psychoanalysis when it is not corrupted (1919, p. 168). Gold is rare but not too rare. The reason for this is connected to its origin. It is a heavy metal formed in supernova explosions in the very far distant past. When a star explodes as a supernova, it scatters its elements throughout the universe. Gold is then collected into the formation of solar systems and planets. Because it is a heavy metal it is collected in the liquid core of a planet like ours and is ejected in volcanic eruptions. It is extruded into seams and accumulates in rivers and streams when it is washed by water from the point of the eruption. Because we still speak of the "bowels of the Earth," maybe we are still aware of a connection between what comes out of them and the shit or filth that shames us.

In spite of this connection with filth, why did painters of the Middle Ages use gold leaf for haloes and why do worshippers in Hindu and Buddhist shrines contribute small amounts of gold leaf to help cover sacred images? Perhaps it shows us the attraction of the products of the bowels in contrast to our civilised distaste. Gold evokes the Sun and the glow of fire which puts it at the heart of religions. The Egyptian god, Ra, for example, had a gold chariot and the throne of the Christian God is usually depicted in gold. All of these activities show the attraction of gold and also demonstrate that it can be used in a religious or spiritual connection as "pure gold" as well as morphing into a symbol of falsehood: "fools" "gold" is only the almost worthless mineral pyrites.

In Part I, Margaret as a therapist does not seem very worried about the pure gold. She works by listening intently and her waiting presence encourages her patient to return to her own thoughts and associations. There is some exchange of thoughts and some provocative statements put into the conversation, like stones in a stream that change the direction of the flow. Mostly, Alice pays for Margaret's time and her benevolent attention. Margaret says little about the transference and does not make much effort to reconstruct the infantile past. With Alice, who is a responsive and well-tuned receiver, Margaret can be facilitative, waiting to see.

Making gold

One of the most interesting and descriptive contributions from the psychological theory developed by Carl Jung lies in his use of the metaphor of alchemy. The alchemists of the Middle Ages spent whole lifetimes in searching for the philosophers' stone, which was imagined as the chemical that would turn base metals into gold. This activity was not always at the fringe of academic activity. Britain's greatest scientist, Isaac Newton, spent a considerable amount of his time on this activity. In effect, it was the form of chemistry that preceded the modern discipline. Experimentation often involved heating a combination of materials in a crucible, then waiting to see what would happen when they mingled with each other at the point of melting. The purpose of this was to find the way to achieve the state in which we will be always in control, the possessor, never the possessed, the giver, never the debtor.

Trust me, I'm a banker

Gold or silver coins were the source of the wealth of Croesus, King of Lydia in 500 BC, and most people have heard the saying "as rich as Croesus." Croesus understood that giving people lumps of gold or silver in exchange for food or cattle was decidedly risky. No-one could tell how pure the supposed gold or silver was and therefore no-one knew just how much they were being given. Croesus thought that issuing coins that were guaranteed to be pure gold and of a standard size and weight would develop trade. His metallurgists devised a technique for purifying gold and making it into small, regularly sized pieces of metal which we have come to call coins. The word "coin" in English is derived from the French "un coin" which means "corner" and refers to the triangular stamps that were used to authenticate the pieces of metal. To show the guaranteed size and purity of these coins, Croesus came up with the idea of stamping all the official coinage with a lion, or parts of a lion to show decreasing value. Trust was now needed only in the ruler who guaranteed the coinage and not in each individual trader; as a result, trade flourished beyond immediate, recognised neighbours. The Egyptians carried on the idea of the guaranteed coin, as did the Chinese, and coins with both faces and inscriptions followed. Statutory regulation of therapists is perhaps an expression of a desire for a standard coinage of reputable therapists.

Paper money was a development that Reiss-Schimmel (1993) ascribes to the growth of trade. Paper money was first developed in China during the seventh century. The routine use of paper money did not reach Europe until the seventeenth century. It was a sign that money could be entirely symbolic, with no possibility that it would be valuable in itself. Paper money developed because merchants travelling far afield needed to be able to carry money for large amounts of goods and could not carry large enough quantities of coins. They needed a trustworthy, convenient, and potent means of exchange. This required an extension of both the capacity to symbolise and the ability to trust. These were the secrets of the success of paper money, which is clearly not worth anything at all but states its principle. British notes, for example, say: "I promise to pay the bearer"; this statement is signed by the Chief Cashier of the Bank of England. The equivalent declaration on US dollar bills is "This note is legal tender for all debts, public and private," signed by the Treasurer of the United States. Few people stop to ask themselves who is making the promise and what their promise is worth.

The term "worth" needs definition and clarification. An object's worth can be expressed in terms of the object for which it could be exchanged. So, for example, a house may be said to be worth so many thousand pounds and that may or may not be the price that it can fetch at the market on a given day. A house has an intrinsic value as well as a market value. The market value is what somebody will actually give in exchange for an object—three beans or a million dollars. The intrinsic worth is what the owner feels that it would be worth if she were to exchange it for something else but it also encompasses a whole train of emotional attachment to the house as a home. Alice, the subject of the case study, is willing to risk a great deal for the sake of pride and self-confidence. Immediately when one begins to think of worth and value, the idea of what someone else will give you enters the equation. With the development of money, risk-taking has become the major question: how much risk is allowed and how much is the potential loss? Is that coin or that note forged? The capacity for taking risks is crucial in all forms of change. Moving forward to the unknown requires trust and a modicum of optimism. We have seen many disasters in the markets because of risk-taking that was not based on sufficient calculation. Patients in therapy may hesitate to entrust themselves to what looks like a risky process.

Trust still has a large part to play in the economies of the twenty first century. Tuckett (2011) has pointed out that the basis of savings, investment, and pensions lies in narratives that must be trusted by the vast majority of those who use them. Information is scant, but stories about what has happened, is happening and will happen are propagated by those who claim to have a position of knowledge. The instability of narratives that are felt to be true but change frequently leads to a felt need to be supported by the law. We see that in some cases, the law stands for the father, actual or imaginary, who can control the power of mother and make the law. This law in financial terms may be expressed in terms of contracts.

A contract is an agreement that is binding in law. Certainly paper money constitutes a form of contract. When I give you a note in return for goods, I am entering a contract with you that is based on the value of the note. The worth of the note depends on the health of the economy that produces it and that means on the good of the guarantor. The importance of that "good" is embedded in the language. A person is "good for nothing" or "good as gold." He can be "as good as his word" and that is the basis of our capitalist society. Alice assumes that she has a contract with Margaret and she would like to know what it is and what it means.

In Great Expectations by Dickens (1860) we can see how the young man, Pip, deceives himself over what he thinks is a contract. He is told that he has "great expectations" and he jumps to the conclusion that his fortune is being assured by the bitter and disillusioned Miss Havisham who means him, he thinks, to marry the beautiful but proud Estella. In fact, she wishes to punish him as a man for the injury that she received from another man who abandoned her on her wedding day. Pip's benefactor is in fact someone else who is marking the trajectory of a gift. In time he will return to claim repayment for his gift. The contract to which Pip commits himself is that he should not investigate the identity of his benefactor and no-one, especially Miss Havisham, wishes to disabuse him. She wishes to see him suffer and his mixture of greed and adolescent love leads him to enter into the contract that dooms him. He is being repaid for his care for the convict but the repayment is no good to him. Pip does not pay the debts that he genuinely owes to the blacksmith who has cared for him and the village girl who genuinely loves him. He rides off with his head in the air and leaves his debts unpaid.

We are all born with a debt. It is expressed by Christianity as original sin and by the saying that we owe God a death; in medicine and psychology the debt is for his life incurred by the infant to his care-givers and sometimes to doctors. Money connects with desire and, as Simmel (1907) pointed out in his argument that money is modernity, it acquires its importance by inserting itself into the teleological chain between a desire and its fulfilment. Money is modern in that it allows us to live our complex lives with interactions in which money circulates from one person to another and usually keeps a standard of value as it goes.

Alice has a feeling that she will have to pay a debt that is more than just the fee that she owes to her therapist. People express this sense of indebtedness in various ways, showing a sense of a day of payment, sometimes expressed as a day of judgment or in the reality of quarter days when rents were due in British and Irish tradition. These linger in the mind as due dates when something will be demanded of us. Alice is not particularly fortunate to begin with; yet a fall from grace is still what she envisages. Patients can express this in all sorts of ways, but for new patients, the invoice and the demand for payment from the therapist is something that is expected, even wanted, and is certainly anticipated.

Money circulates and goes from one person to another taking with it much more than the power to purchase. Money has equated with status over the ages. The old regime tried hard to maintain the idea that birth and education are more important than money, as the scorn in the term *nouveau riche* demonstrates. Status is still demonstrated by money or at least by purchasing power. The middle classes have always been over-awed by large houses and the paraphernalia of wealth, as Alice discovered in her experience of a private school and an Oxbridge college. Man seems to be a hierarchical animal and social class is of great importance to each person's sense of herself. Money may or may not be available, but somewhere in the background of a person from the upper classes in western society there is likely to have been education and, even in the post-war welfare state of the UK, education has required to be backed by a certain amount of money. For the child, as the young Alice shows, lack of money is a source of shame because it is felt as a quality of the self that may be exposed in all sorts of ways, not as something that has been done or not done.

Money, gifts, and debt

Most people like to be seen as generous. This can give us problems because we may also need to be able to receive gifts. The person who says "You shouldn't have" when given something is not just trying to end the chain of obligation, but is also letting the donor know that receiving is difficult. The reluctant recipient might add consciously or unconsciously to the phrase, making it: "You shouldn't have, because now I will have to pay you back." In other words, a gift is felt to create a debt. Because of this, expensive gifts are felt to be a burden that must be repaid so that there can be a return to a state of nothing owed.

Why is debt so uncomfortable? Freud has the explanation that his theory implies: it makes us feel powerless. As the creditor, you can demand goods and services from the debtor. In ordinary life, you have the moral upper hand. You may be magnanimous and forgive a debt or, like Shylock in The Merchant of Venice, you may demand its exact repayment. An excessively narcissistic person will feel entitled to have all repayments made to him or her. In marriage, unfaithfulness is often felt to imply a state of indebtedness in which the wronged partner may demand that the other should make amends. Whether this debt is honoured and for how long will be crucial to the relationship. In the twenty-first century, we see celebrities feeling entitled to satisfaction, refusing to tolerate unfaithfulness and ending relationships, whereas less famous people who come for psychotherapy are more likely to prolong the relationship while seeking to exact the debt that the behaviour seems to have accrued. The success or failure of the relationship depends on how each party deals with the power imbalance created by the debt.

This kind of debt has its roots in giving. The unfaithful partner, whose actions form so many narratives, gives something of him or herself to another outside the relationship and this gift creates the debt. Marriage settlements were the vehicle by which fathers ensured that their daughters would not be left penniless by a feckless or unfaithful husband. Now prenuptial agreements are often required in order to ensure a fair distribution of wealth if a relationship breaks down. These enforce the giving and the payment of debts but generosity requires trust and an openness which not everyone has had the opportunity to develop.

The trajectory of money in society ensures that we are dealing with circularity. In earning, stealing, or appropriating money, we take something that does not yet belong to us but has already been possessed by someone else. We all know that money stays only temporarily and then it will stay with someone else to whom it will not belong. We may go to extraordinary lengths to convince ourselves that it does belong and that is where pathology begins.

Pathology or suffering begins when the relationship to money is troublesome to the individual or interferes with human relationships. We can empathise with the problems of relationship but it is harder to empathise with the love of money. Why can a girl sing of her lost love, but a miser cannot sing of his lost money? Brenner (1986) postulates that (if this is true) it is because we can enter into the feeling of the girl but not the miser. This is a powerful debate because it illuminates the social context in which loving money can be shameful and is considered to be only a substitute for loving a human object.

Greed

Human beings have needed food and then wanted comfort and stimulation since they began to work together and specialise in skills and tasks. Acquiring and saving money may be easier than saving goods but greed, or inordinate appetite, is apparent with any litter of animals where the greediest gets the most food and survives but the runt gets thinner and may die. This explains an ambivalent attitude towards appetite.

Great literary figures of the past saw that money is one of the most powerful signifiers for western European humanity. The Bible tells us that the love of money is the root of all evil (1Timothy 10). For Geoffrey Chaucer, the teaching of the Bible was so much a part of the air that he breathed that he gave the Pardoner a tale in his Canterbury Tales that demonstrates the destructive power of the love of money. The Pardoner was an employee of the Roman Catholic Church in the Middle Ages who was authorised to wander the country like a tinker but, rather than selling pots and pans, he was selling pardons that would excuse people from time to be spent in Purgatory expiating their sins. The amount of money paid would be linked to a specific length of time that could be remitted. The practice of buying pardons was discredited and abolished in the Reformation, but it demonstrates the importance of money as a signifier of power. The sinner who had money could buy himself a pass that would get him into heaven sooner, in spite of whatever crimes or sins he might have committed. In this way both shame and guilt could be circumvented.

Providing power, whether illusory or practical, is one of the most important roles played by money in the mind. Money comes to symbolise the power that the infant lacks. For the French psychoanalyst, Lacan (1966a), understanding and deepening of the ideas of Sigmund Freud meant that although money as a pile of gold may be important, the true significance of "money" is implicated in the word and all that it brings with it as a signifier which Lacan says represents the subject to another signifier. In other words, I can explain what a word means to me only by the use of other words. I need more signifiers to represent me to you. Signifiers are all linked to each other and form a signifying chain for any subject or individual seeking to speak. Money however is a unique signifier in that "it is always lacking and precisely to the extent that one possesses it since loss is inscribed in its very possession which explains why one can never have enough of it." (Arnaud, 2003, p. 30)

The Pardoner in Geoffrey Chaucer's The Canterbury Tales provides an interesting signifying train. He is a villain according to his own description of his activities, selling people fake relics and pocketing the money that they pay him for indulgences. Yet he tells an uplifting and totally acceptably moral tale about the corrupting power of money. The story is of three rogues who set out on a drunken spree after one of their friends has died. They decide to look for Death in order to defeat it, just as those who come to the Pardoner seek to do. They come upon an old man who tells them that they will find Death under a certain tree. When they get there they find a pile of gold coins. They immediately want to take the coins but decide that they had better wait until dark. They draw lots to send one of the three to the town to buy food and drink while the other two wait. The two who are waiting decide to kill the third when he returns and he decides to poison the wine that he brings back. These plans are all carried out and all of them find death under the tree.

Money in this story provides a deadly attraction or even perhaps a correlate of the self-destructive instinct. Sigmund Freud thought a great deal about our relationship with death. His argument about death was that all living cells seek to return to a state of rest or homeostasis. This sounds anthropomorphic but was based in his understanding of mechanics as well as biology (1920b).

In 'The Pardoner's Tale' the symbolism is connected to myth and fairy tale. Chaucer's story echoes the power of the oracle in Greek society. The oracle speaks a kind of truth but usually in a very enigmatic and mysterious form. The only way to act on it was to come to a conclusion about its meaning and then to seek to avoid what it appeared to be warning about. In many myths, the conclusion reached by the protagonist is too literal. Chaucer's three rogues rush headlong into their fate because they are greedy and because they do not understand the symbolic. In Freud's terms, they fulfil their fundamental instinctual need to find Death. For them, Death is a person whom they can seek to destroy. Those who confuse the literal with the symbolic are doomed to fail to be able to deal with either.

The attraction of money

Freud was interested in why we are so attracted to money. For the analytical therapist the answer is not a simple matter of wanting to exchange it for desirable things. Why, for example, do misers hoard money that they can never bring themselves to spend? Freud's answer was that there is a certain group of people who share three main characteristics: they display avarice, pedantry, and obstinacy (Freud, 1917). What we can usually see in these people would be an emphasis on order and control with particular attention to cleanliness. Listening to the thoughts of the people with this group of qualities led Freud to think that perhaps these people are defending against the opposite. Perhaps they are people with a particular interest in dirt and disorder.

> Wherever the archaic way of thinking has prevailed or still prevails in the old civilisations, in myths, fairy tales superstition or unconscious thinking in dreams and in neuroses, money has been brought into the closest connection with filth. (1924, p. 169)

Freud in 1917 had explored the character of the small child's fascination with his own faeces as a sort of delight in possession. This is perhaps the first thing that the child truly owns. He can then give it up to his mother as a gift even though he learns that she just throws it away. Here is the origin of the ambivalent attitude to money displayed most strongly in those who have not moved on from the struggle over holding on and letting go. Alice's husband, Oliver, shows some of these qualities. He seeks refuge in work and in the paper that he has to finish. He retreats to his study where he hoards papers and likes to be surrounded by his own sort of untidiness. A physical illness confronts him with his lack of control over his own body. Of course, this distresses everyone but is perhaps worse for someone with an obsessional temperament.

People who display these qualities may take pleasure in possessing money for its own sake, not in spite of its connection with filth, but because of it. Alice herself shows an attachment to money because it gives her a sense of security. She scrabbles in the earth to produce something worthwhile eventually but for the moment it is a way of focussing on what is in front of her rather than what is inside her. Out of the earth can come flowers or vegetables but Alice has not reached that point yet.

People who are interested in the earth (dirt in American English) are also likely to be interested in the process of giving and receiving. The small children who are achieving control of their bowels may want to be able to make a gift but will see that the first gift is just thrown away and so may be considered to be of no value. Hence the position of the miser arises: "If I keep it all for myself, that is the only way that I will know that my money is appreciated, even loved." Here is the origin of the ambivalent attitude to money displayed most strongly in those who have not moved on from the anal stage. (See Chapter xx). They will take pleasure in possessing money for its own sake, not in spite of its connection with filth, but because of it.

Alice wants to be able to see that her therapist grows something valuable from the soil in her garden. This for her will be a symbol of the therapist being able to transform the dirt into the beautiful. The story of Alice shows us that money in itself, not just as a symbol, may not be the first thing that is negotiated in psychotherapy but sooner or later it will have to be faced as a medium of exchange. She is however, concerned about what she can offer to her therapist and whether she will be good enough as a patient. She was not told that she would have to pay for her first session and she receives it as a sort of gift. Gifts as we shall see later are a mixed blessing and lead to mixed emotions in the recipient. Alice is not sure what rights of possession she has or what she can impose on her therapist. Some patients can deal with this level of anxiety but others will find it difficult to endure.

Use it or lose it

Because money taunts us with the possibility of possession, it brings up another aspect of Freud's theory: he found that both boys and men begin to fear the loss of the penis through castration and that this fear takes many forms and many directions in adult emotional life. He pointed out that the little boy discovers that girls and women do not have penises and therefore he deduces that it is a detachable part of the body. He has already discovered that faeces are a detachable part of the body and for this reason he begins to form the equation that the penis and the faeces are in some way equivalent. He also learns that babies are expelled from the body just as faeces are, thus completing the symbolic equation: faeces = penis = baby.

Oliver has to accept that his cancer is attacking his genitals and that this is the focus of his masculinity. He is likely to express defences that show his anxiety about his loss or potential loss of his manhood. To Alice, he is more enigmatic than ever in both his withdrawal from her and his critical, attacking behaviour. She may be able to think about his needs and his anxiety but her reminiscences at first are about the gentleness of her father and although she does not mention the contrast, it may have been in her mind. Her therapist might need to highlight this for her if she is not able to see it for herself.

Where does this leave money in the psychopathology of women and men? For a man, money may represent the penis which he fears to lose. As a child enters the phallic phase of development, the phallus which is a more general term for the imaginary and symbolic functions of the penis will at times be represented by the power of money. Feminists will also argue that for a woman, money may represent phallic power and therefore be even more important to her than it is for the man who actually possesses the penis which also represents the phallus. He will seek to amass as much money as possible and to hold on to it, out of fear that it can be taken away from him. She will seek to have a man with money or to have money of her own. She could have both the symbols of phallic power. As money represents his masculinity to a man, he will resist as strongly and fiercely as he can if he is threatened with its loss. On the other hand, money will also represent the gift that he as a small child can give his mother and the gift of a baby that he can give to his partner. He will therefore be held in a tension between generosity and miserliness which may be resolved in different ways at different times with the help of the culture and society in which he lives and by the nature of the women he knows.

As this argument suggests, Freud has not provided a convincing theory for women and desire. What will keep a woman in check if she has already lost her phallic power? The psychoanalyst, Horney (1922) provided a view of women's desire that allowed for the woman to desire power that the penis symbolises rather than the penis itself. The feminists who followed her were not slow to point out the importance of phallic power as distinct from anatomy, but the argument is not yet over and Jacques Lacan who saw the phallus as signifier of the lack of the Other has carried the debate to a new level in his idea that woman equals lack. As a universal concept, she does not even exist: "la femme n'existe pas." (1973, p. 60).

Generosity

Most people like to be seen as generous. The patient who has difficulties with giving and receiving may try to offer too much money to his therapist. "Too much" is defined as the amount that he will not be able to maintain for the length of time that he needs to. He may do this in order to avoid the sense of debt. The person who feels shamed by receiving a gift will try to be always in the position of the giver.

In therapy this can be addressed as a sense of shame. The patient is not able to feel that he is worth much unless he can supplement himself with gifts.

Of course gifts can simply express gratitude. Klein (1959) found that the capacity for love and gratitude followed the decline of the paranoid position and the ability to remain in the depressive position. The therapist must find her own way of thinking about gifts as both healthy and desirable, evoking gratitude and also an expression of submission which needs interpreting. Freud (1917) looks to the anal elements of character and points out that

> those who question this derivation of gifts should consider their experience of psychoanalytic treatment, study the gifts they receive as doctors from their patients and watch the storms of transference which a gift from them can rouse in their patients. (1917, p. 299)

Money and words

Forrester (1997) has written of the extent to which speech and all the exchanges that make up language pass from one to another of us and are accepted on trust to mean more or less what they say. Yet sometimes language, like a coin, can be a forgery, can lose its face, and be effaced. Clichés, for example, are devalued coinage that can no longer carry the value that they originally bore. We recognise them sometimes but one man's cliché might be another's new metaphor. Perhaps it is the promise in the contract that it is important. If the person offering the coin is honest and has the goods to back it up, all may be well. On the other hand, a debased coinage is recognisable in empty speech, the words that do not carry the full emotional value that they should have. They are still the representations of debts.

Jacques Lacan wrote of the importance of "full speech" that carries its full weight and value of emotion. Forrester speaks also of "responsible" and "irresponsible" speech. In the consulting room we can speak without responsibility, not worrying so much about the censor in the head, which tells us all not to speak of this or that and not to speak in this or that profane or angry way. In everyday life, we speak usually with some responsibility and sometimes conscious thought of the impact of our speech on others. The contracts are different with different people.

When they form psychoanalytic theory, words imply a debt. All those of us who make use of Freud's thinking "owe him a debt." This would be a common speech formulation that conceals the truth which is that Freud's thinking circulates like currency and does not stay with any one of us. When a concept moves on, like a penny, it takes all sorts of finger prints, grime, and bacteria with it. I have to recognise that I have altered it by possessing it temporarily. We recognise the effect of circulation. It enables us to gain goods and even ideas that we want and need but it also passes on evils like falsehood and perhaps disease and even death. Circulation takes money away from each person but also brings new possibilities. It leaves us owing debts to each other but it inscribes us more closely in a social order.

CHAPTER EIGHT

Growing in relation to money

This chapter will describe a development in the infant's relation to the world and to others which correlates to his relationship to money, as he moves from a system of gifts to barter and then to a system of trust and symbolic transaction. In therapy too, the adult progresses through a developmental trajectory towards greater trust and faith in his or her own humanity. She can allow herself to be in another's debt and becomes able to treat her own debtors with generosity. The new-born infant opens her eyes to a blinding light, noise, and sensations all over her body that are all entirely new. Modern birthing processes allow for a little shielding of the baby from the shock of the first experience of the world outside the relative safety of the womb. Whatever the birth experience, the new-born has more to learn than any adult can imagine. Seeing a child change from the innocence of this first minute to become the standing, walking, individual who is beginning to begin to talk at the end of the first year is one of the most moving experiences of the miraculous that anyone can have.

The gift economy

The English word economy is derived from the Greek word oikonomia that refers to the management of the household and it has kept some of that meaning in English although Smith (1750) related it to the management of the resources of a state. In a relationship, we can apply it to the management of resources and the extent to which each person feels satisfied and has needs met. In that sense we can refer to an economy that develops in each family, beginning with the man and the woman or partners coming together so that there can be a mother or primary carer and a baby. Once this happens, the individual's experience is affected by the management of his or her resources, which involves the balancing of income and expenditure and the currency that is valid for the members of the family for moving resources around.

Much work is now being done by neuroscientists and psychotherapists and on the process that enables the baby to learn. Current research is based on the work of earlier researchers like Spitz (1965) and John Bowlby (1975) among others who made it clear that affective relationships whether with one caregiver or an increasing number are crucial for all forms of emotional and cognitive development. One of the obvious qualities of the early relationship will be determined by the mother's attitude to feeding. There is or is not enough milk. There is or is not enough money to buy food. The infant begins to sense the adults' attitude to needs and begins to form an attitude to her own demands. The quality of the relationship that the mother and others who are close are able to establish with the child will enable her to develop her own unique mental capacities.

The small child is embedded in the gift economy of the early months in which gifts are exchanged and may become conditional, for example, on good behaviour. The point at which conditionality enters the process is a moment at which the child begins to enter a more adult order. In most families there are overt conditions set for rewards and punishments. Mothers are inclined to reward smiles and a responsive baby with more frequent contact and more holding and verbalising. One young mother sat in a chair beside the cot, holding her baby aged about three months and read her stories. Clearly, there was no way the baby could understand Winnie the Pooh but she loved the sound of her mother's voice and she provided the rewards of solemn attention and eye contact, followed in due course by smiles.

The gift economy therefore begins to have an element of barter of the order: "I will smile at you if you give me your nipple." There has not been a historical example of a society wholly based on barter even though there are still examples such as North American Indians who bring rugs and baskets to trading posts to exchange for groceries and other necessities. This kind of market in turn develops into the market economy. The laws of supply and demand dominate the market and the child begins to learn about the limits of supply and the pain of demand. In the market the child begins to trust the adult to keep a promise. Tuckett (2011) emphasises that the financial markets of the twenty-first century work only because of a general belief in the narratives that we are given and that we accept. The trust in other people to deliver good outcomes that begins to develop in the infant will enable him to participate in the adult world. First, however, the child needs to learn that absent objects can be found. Freud described this process as the "fort da" game. He watched his eighteen-month-old grandson playing with a cotton reel on a string. The baby dropped the cotton reel over the edge of the cot so that he could not see it saying something like "ooo" or fort ("gone" in German) and when he pulled it back again he would say da ("there" in German) and Freud made the important observation that there is a point in development when the child looks for an absent cotton reel when, for example, he hid it under the carpet. Earlier on, the younger child does not look. Out of sight is out of mind. This ability to remember and conceptualise an object and hold it in mind when it is absent is a developmental achievement. This stage is a pre requisite to symbolisation and is a pre requisite to being able to wait for a promise to be fulfilled. One patient described her family myth that she was parked in the garden in a pram because her mother believed that fresh air was good for the baby in any weather. Her mother told her cheerfully that she cried herself to exhaustion and had to be parked out of earshot. Her mother had always seemed pleased with this and said it had taught my patient to wait for satisfaction and in particular to save up for anything that she wanted and not to expect to get it immediately.

As they develop memory, babies may learn to wait in hope rather than in blind despair. James and Joyce Robertson, two British psychoanalysts, made a documentary film for the Tavistock Institute called John, aged seventeen months, for nine days in a residential nursery (Robertson & Robertson, 1969). John's mother had to go into hospital to have a second baby. The film's summary reads (Robertson Films, 2011):

For two days John tries to attach himself to a nurse, but because they are not assigned to individual children no nurse attends to John long enough to understand him and answer his needs. He is not mothered or protected from attacks by the other children. Food and routines are strange, and the father's visits can do little to ease the situation. John becomes increasingly distressed, and eventually sinks into hopeless apathy. At reunion he rejects his mother.

The film shows the difficulty for a child when a promise is not kept. John was a toddler and could clearly hold an image of his mother. When she did not return, his despair is painful to watch and the film shows the stages of his hope turning to loss and depression. This shows among many other things that a child has a sense of trust and hope which can be damaged when the implied promise of his mother's return is broken. The Robertsons' research on separation of mothers and children in hospitals led to a change of hospital practice in Britain so that in the present-day system the hospital encourages a parent to stay with the child in hospital if at all possible.

We know that many adults see no necessity to keep promises to small children. The harassed mother in the supermarket who promises sweets to the child who will behave himself will probably keep her part of the bargain because she still has to drive home and the screaming toddler who has been denied his promised reward will make driving dangerous. But what if he didn't earn his reward or if there was a dispute about whether he earned it? This situation in the therapeutic relationship is not easy to negotiate. The patient attends his sessions, pays his fees, and expects to feel better. As we know, gratification is delayed in this respect and after an initial period of euphoria arising from catharsis or the gratification of attention, the demands for the redemption of the non-existent promissory note may begin through clear demands, acting in and out and sometimes in metaphorical or symbolic howling.

The crying baby at the beginning expresses everything in the same way as far as a stranger can tell. From the point of view of her mother or primary carer, her cries begin to be decipherable into pain or anger, and gradually into other more complex areas of distress. At this stage, the infant is totally dependent on his mother. From her he receives everything as a gift. This is assuming a normal expectable mother with an adequately healthy baby. Titmuss (1970), in a study that examined economic, sociological, and psychological factors, described the process of giving blood in the United States as a gift relationship. The mother of a new born baby forms a gift relationship with her baby which has something in common with the person who is donating blood. She is in the same way a selected and special person who is able to make this gift. She is doing it partly from altruism because of the need of her help-less small baby. She is also doing it out of motives that relate to her own interests as is the blood donor. In so far as the baby is felt to be a part of her own body, she will usually defend it, protect it and nourish it as though it were her better self. Titmuss concluded in his study that some people donate blood to protect themselves or their families from future need. Some mothers might be motivated by this feeling for fam-ily relationship and, probably at an unconscious level, some may be motivated by a wish for the preservation of their own blood line and genetic heritage.

Whatever her motivation, a good enough mother gives her gifts of milk, protection and general physical care out of an altruism that often demands no response but may include an awareness of the possibility of a response that will come later. The very young infant may make eye contact and will almost from the beginning recognise a human face as more interesting than other aspects of its environment. She will recognise her own mother's smell and she may be able to recognise the voice from the pre-natal experience and will often show a prefer-ence for being held by her mother rather than a stranger or even her father, from an early stage. All these are small offerings from the infant to the mother but the first main gift that the infant is able to give will be her smile. The smile is immensely important in the relationship and marks the point at which there is an exchange. The smile is both intrin-sically valuable to the mother and also symbolic because it stands for the baby's potential to relate and to become a person who will speak. Most mothers scrutinise the baby's face for the first signs of the muscle movements of a smile and are proud and delighted when they are sure that they are seeing a genuine smile, not a grimace. From that moment on, ordinary healthy mothers will seek to evoke smiles as often as they can. Imitation seems to play a considerable part in the development of this early communication and mothers will smile and coo at the infant in frequent attempts to evoke the desired response. Complete strangers, on trains, for example, will do the same, seeking to evoke the baby's attention and delight.

The exchange economy

At this point, we could say that there is the beginning of an exchange economy in which one gift is balanced by a reciprocal gift. In the early stages it is not yet an exchange as one gift does not depend on the other. Only a mother who is very disturbed will punish a small baby for not smiling, but there can be little doubt that the infant who smiles readily will give enjoyment to her mother that makes it more likely that she will be picked up and fed and less likely that she will be left to cry for long periods. Even grandparents and friends will ask if they may pick up the baby and this is more likely to be rewarding and therefore reinforced if the baby smiles. Of course the opposite may also be true. The grandmother who does not receive smiles may be much more energetic in holding and vocalising to the baby in order to encourage her development and ensure that she is progressing normally.

There are many ways of conceptualising development in human beings. Theory developed in the last part of the twentieth and early twenty-first centuries has given much attention to narcissism and the development of a secure sense of self and other. The infant may be thought to be encapsulated in a primary narcissism at the beginning but will be perhaps moving into relationship as she begins to make eye contact. The narcissistic economy begins to develop as the child is able to see and recognise others.

Understanding value

Children begin by thinking that any coin can buy any goods. A sense of value develops over time. Some coins will buy more than others. Some things cannot be bought by any number of coins that the child is likely to have, or cannot be bought at all. For the child there is a whole world of power in the money that parents possess and can give or withhold. The child learns that money itself has power and the power of money is related to the adult assessment of value. From the beginning, the child's value system relates directly to pleasure. The toy that he or she likes, and the old blanket that has been loved as a transitional object with its own smell and familiarity is worth everything; the expensive newly bought doll may be worth nothing. Of course adults also have value systems that do not relate directly to monetary value. Advertising science involves persuading people that what is expensive is also valuable. The child gradually begins to understand that these two systems are different. The latency child is likely to desire whatever his culture regards as valuable. He is affected by advertising and by peer pressure and gradually his desire moves into the socially expected range for his age and gender. There are of course exceptions. Some children retain their own value systems and do not want electronic gadgets or games and keep their sights fixed on a violin or a dancing lesson. As the child comes to recognise his own desires, he is either confirmed as a member of his social group or he takes up a place on the edge or outside a group altogether.

The process of recruiting young people for the radical fringes of religion is based on their desire for a clear value system which fits the idealism of youth and preferably gives motivation for action which seals the sense of belonging. For some people the call to terrorism is based on valuing a mistaken interpretation of religious imperatives above the ordinary value system of the culture and society to which they belong. This mistaken value system, a form of méconnaissance gives a sense of knowing the truth that leads to a superiority which is difficult to change. Knowing the truth and being right can lead to self-exclusion from the main economy. An example of this is the radicalisation of the young Hassan who is recruited for terrorism in the novel A Week in December by Faulks (2009). He is taught to despise the consumerism of the capitalist economy and then to go to the length of trying to kill some of those who participate in it.

Use of symbols

Since money represents goods or services, it functions as a symbol and no-one can manipulate money or its equivalent until they are able to use and interpret symbols at least at a basic level. The process by which an individual enters this order of thinking and communicating has preoccupied psychoanalytic theorists. Jacques Lacan charted the course of the development of the ego through his major paper on the mirror stage: Le Stade du Miroir (1966b). He took the moment at which the baby recognises herself in a mirror and is delighted with the image as a demonstration that the ego mistakes its own weakness for beauty and strength. The baby is still helpless and is supported by the arms of an adult but she responds to an idealised image of herself. In this we can all recognise the méconnaisssance of our own omnipotence that persists into adulthood. From this moment we are subject to all the dangers of a delusional sense of power leading to manic relationships with the objects of the outside world including money.

Of course the opposite kind of delusion is also possible. Many people have developed a cruel and inadequate self-image in which value is not based on the individual's potential or contribution to family or society but instead is based on another judgment, usually formed in the past as a reaction to a relationship. Very often this is traceable to a parent or significant carer but is also frequently related to a brother or sister. Coles (2003) believed that the image that siblings feed back to the young child can be important in forming a self-image:

> I believe there is a relationship between an unjustly harsh superego and the experience of sibling cruelty. (2003, p. 12)

Parents unintentionally make this phenomenon worse by favouring one child, often the youngest who is then hated by the older children for seeming to have an unfair share of the parents' love. In later life this is often symbolised in legacies. "He never loved me as much and he has left me less than he left you which proves it." These family feuds after death of a parent can be most painful and destructive but they also shine a light on some of the causative factors of shame and lack of confidence. The earliest experiences may never have been expressed in words and may show themselves only in behaviour patterns in the present.

Therapy enables words to be found for early experiences. Children have very different experiences of entering the domain of language. For Jacques Lacan this is not a straightforward linear development. Once the ego has made its first narcissistic error, the child is ready to enter the world of language where there is an infinite universe of signifiers. There cannot be a "before" because we can think about what went before only by using the very signifiers that we are examining. For this reason, Lacan thought that the study of development is outside the realm of psychoanalysis. However that may be, the child enters the world of language and becomes subject to it, able to think what his language enables him to think. He can recognise that the word "book" can evoke a book when no book is present. He has discovered loss and lack. Very importantly for his learning, he can understand as he grows that a coin can represent sweets or a new game or anything that he desires. When he possesses coins he has power. The dawning of understanding of the nature of money is therefore an accompaniment to his discovery of his own power and the power of others. Understanding of the power and limitation of money progresses along with the use of symbols. Language usually develops accurate syntax and complexity during the third and fourth years.

The two or three-year-old child passes through the stage of learning to control his excretion as well as many other social restraints and requirements. These are culturally determined but all human societies and many animals also have customary processes and places for excretion and do not allow their young to foul their nests or holes or dens. Some of the higher mammals as well as birds use fairly sophisticated sounds that function as communication, inviting, warning, or alerting and can perform tasks for rewards but we can question whether any of them has the same capacity as humans to use a sound as a symbol of an object.

Symbolising therefore is a largely but not uniquely human skill. The effect of language is to remove the necessity for relating to objects directly. A cow can be represented by the word "cow," by £100 or a bag of magic beans. Most children begin to use words themselves at the end of the first year although they may understand words spoken to them before that. Chimpanzees have recently been studied and the film of Nim (Project Nim, 2011) indicates that a chimpanzee may be able to learn sign language, a process which does require symbolisation. Some parents find that using Sign Language helps babies to express themselves more intelligibly before they can use words. Signs such as "more" or "drink" can be recognised and attempted before the muscular control of the vocal organs is sufficiently mature for words to be articulated. The importance of imitation is difficult to over emphasise and it is clearly operative in this process.

Imitation plays an even more major role in human development than had been understood by psychoanalysis although it has a long human history and was clear to Shakespeare. René Gerard wrote of mimetic or imitative desire in the genesis of love; "when mimetic desire is thwarted it intensifies and when it succeeds it withers away." (1991, p. 34) The lovers in A Midsummer Night's Dream learn that love is catching and can perhaps be caught:

Oh teach me how you look and by what art
You sway the motion of Demetrius heart. (Act I, Scene i,
    pp. 292–293)

Attitudes to the use and misuse of money will similarly be at least in part mimetic. The child watches her significant adults. Alice saw her parents and grandparents worrying about money in her childhood where money was clearly a problem for her parents and she is susceptible to similar anxieties herself. Of course, in both the case of adult sexual love and in the case of worrying about money, we can see that it is a matter of reason as well as learned attitude and behaviour. If money becomes a matter of life and death for Alice, we would expect high levels of realistic anxiety to help her to find the courage to act.

This chapter has looked at the developmental process by which the child's self-absorption is modified so that she can relate to another human being and can develop her sense of herself. She can then develop her values and the process by which objects and other people can be assessed. Tracking the process by which one begins to look outwards at other people in order to make exchanges and to give and receive is one way of looking at the changes that take place as the child takes her place in the economy of her inner world, her family, and her culture.

CHAPTER NINE

Spendthrift or miser?

The small-scale exchanges of the infant and young child lead the way towards the exchange economy in which the adult lives. This chapter will concentrate on the external effects of the child's struggle for control of ingestion and excretion, showing how each person reveals an attitude to holding on or letting go, getting and spending and how that relates to his place in society and the presenting problem that he might bring to therapy. Aspects of the financial markets are an indicator of social attitudes to money as are more intimate relationships with partners and other family members. The mass media are interested in the divorce settlements of celebrities and hold discussions on the rights of spouses and civil partners. Each adult is a potential or actual partner in a relationship of some sort whether in a marriage or at work or within a family.

The social context

Ever since Freud published Civilisation and its discontents in 1930, citing guilt and the destructive instinct as the two main forces dominating our social relationships, writers thinkers have used psychoanalytic theory to clarify human and social behaviour. In relation to money and its impact on the individual, social structures are important in reinforcing the guilt that the individual will construct for himself. Freud began this work with a statement about value:

> It is impossible to escape the impression that people commonly use false standards of measurement—that they seek power, success and wealth for themselves and admire them in others and that they underestimate what is of true value in life. (1930, p. 1)

Freud was writing of value which in some ways is a much more difficult concept than currency. The usual definition of value is given by the Oxford English Dictionary as "the extent to which on object can be exchanged for another." Yet we also speak of "intrinsic" value which in the context of ethics is an attempt to remove the idea of exchange and to imply an end to the signifying chain. Intrinsic worth need go no further but concentrates upon itself as subject and object.

Karl Marx on the other hand wrote that both the subject and the object are implicated in the meaning and role of money. "That which mediates my life for me also mediates other people" (1844, p. 120). Recapitulating the theme of destructiveness, Karl Marx was interested in the extent to which the worker is alienated from the product of his labour. The product of his work is appropriated by the capitalist and he is given back only as much as the bosses decide. The State has also to take its share as taxation as well as often acting in the role of employer. At the beginning of the twenty-first century we seem to be entering a period of instability and unrest over who controls the sources of wealth. Destructiveness can follow deprivation.

There must be an almost infinite number of ways in which money and its symbolic equivalents impinge on our lives both as individuals and in groups, but the two themes of destructiveness and guilt are representative enough to demonstrate the ways in which the social context will show itself in the consulting room.

Destructiveness through theft

Novels, like plays, hold the mirror up to nature and often provide a useful case study to set against the story of Alice. Silas Marner was published in 1861 by Mary Ann Evans (Eliot, 1861), writing under the male nom de plume, "George Eliot," because of the failure to take women writers seriously at the time. It is a novel about morality, religious and social bigotry and the symbolic power of money. She plays with the attraction of money and shows both its power to enslave and over turn morality and its consoling, reassuring quality. Both guilt and destructiveness enter into the relationships with money of individuals and communities.

One of the Ten Commandments in the Old Testament is "Thou shalt not steal" (Exodus 20, 17). This central position gives us some indication of the importance of property in human social development. The baby begins from an assumption that everything is mine or at least that there is no sense in which anything is not mine. For an infant the breast belongs to him and is him. His own development and experience lead him to understand that it is actually under the control of a separate person. From then on, the question of property rights matters to each one of us. The school child fights for her pencil case and her mobile phone when another child tries to take it. Adults move on to more demanding relationships with property, buying cars and houses which can cost many times their annual earnings. The relationship with these possessions begins to equate to a relationship to debt for most people. Owning a house differs from other personal property. Most Americans do not own the land on which their houses are built according to Thom McEvoy which might show us a certain precariousness in the relationship of property to the land on which it stands (McEvoy, 2001, p. 41). Individuals can own the house but the land belongs to the state. This symbolises the sense in which we have some rights of ownership but they are balanced on top of a substrate which we can never own. Money is a temporary possession of this sort. It is an iceberg of which we normally only ever see the outermost tip in the form of the cash that we handle. Most people deal with large amounts of money, if they need to, through electronic media or the paper medium of a cheque.

Possession implies the possibility of loss. Imagining the loss of money can grow into a monstrous but intangible experience that may be based on fraud and our own stupidity. Fraud is punished more severely than theft. Socially, we are more concerned with the disruption of order and trust than by circulation which will happen anyway (Arnaud, 2003). The victim might have given away a password or a key that leaves him open to theft. This fear connects with a sense of shame. A broad general background of anxiety contrasts with the specific fear of losses through burglary or mugging which also worries those who own property although anxiety usually develops to an acute state only after a personal experience or in states of internal distress.

Theft and loss

The fear of theft may also be rooted in the fear of other losses which might differ for each person but might also have some common features. In Freudian theory, the underlying fear to track is the fear of castration. The man becomes aware that he is capable of losing what the woman has already lost. The feminist view is that the woman may have phallic power even if she does not have a penis and that she is just as capable of fearing the loss of this phallus as is the man. All adults are afraid of losing control of themselves and others. The flow of money in and out is a reassuring reminder that some control is in place.

In order to understand the psychological basis for theft we can look immediately at envy and that is often a consciously accessible part of the motivation. When groups of people riot and loot, an obvious assumption is that they suffered from envy and wanted to have what others have or to destroy what they cannot have. This is often one strand of the emotion but there are many others. There is excitement and the pleasure of acting as a group as well as defiance of authority. Someone who is at the developmental stage of dealing with defiance of his father might be particularly susceptible to these temptations.

George Eliot puts theft at the beginning of *Silas Marner* and shows how it sets in motion a train of enforced emotional consequences for the youth in a social group. At the beginning of the novel, Marner, a young man who is a solitary weaver, is betrayed by his best friend who steals the money of a dying mutual friend and pins the blame on Silas. All his friends in his religious community at Lantern Yard abandon him and the girl he was to marry writes to break off the engagement. Another's greed for money has brought about his downfall and left him isolated and alone. The values of this group are shown to be "a false standard of measurement" since they immediately forget what they know of Marner and the goodness and charity of his life, including his willingness to sit with the dying man and they show that they are ready to exclude him.

Eliot then uses money as a signifier that runs through the novel. Marner's mother taught him to use foxgloves to make a remedy for the heart complaint known as dropsy. He gives it to a neighbour to ease her distress and she is immediately relieved of her symptoms. This act of generosity is in direct contrast with the greed and selfishness of his friend William's behaviour towards him. He becomes known in the area for his herbal remedies and although there is risk in this of being seen as a servant of the devil, people are happy to give him money for his services, and he acquires a store of money that he is very loath to spend. He finds the money comforting and Eliot describes the way he takes out the coins and talks to them, making them into a companion in his lonely life. Even though it shown in a sympathetic light, he is shown to be measuring by false standards but he has tried to love his neighbours and been rejected.

Eliot makes money symbolise a complex of elements of Silas Marner's life. As the fruit of his labours, it represents for him the warmth and love of other people. He is not able to express himself and no-one is likely to listen to him if he tries to say that he has been wronged and that he would like to be reinstated in his place in his church in Lantern Yard. His human kindness is expressed in the good deeds that he is still able to do for his neighbours but the only reward that he receives for his kindness is the money that he accumulates.

Money is the reward for Marner's craft and his labour and stands in place of human kindness:

> The weaver's hand had known the touch of hard-won money even before the palm had grown to its full breadth; for twenty years mysterious money had stood to him as the symbol of earthly good and the immediate object of toil.

He has no sense that there is anything dirty or unacceptable about gold. In fact he also has a relationship with a brown pot which he used to fetch his water from the well. It is a satisfying shape which we might think has something of the female about it and he loved to caress it. One day he broke it and he grieved for its loss. This very poignant account shows that we can consider Marner to be beyond the stage in which the whole world is part of him. He is capable of a loving relationship that is not reciprocated but is not rejected either, even though the woman he was to marry has been driven away by the stench created by the evil of William's behaviour.

Eliot shows an understanding of the power of money at several levels. At first, Marner enjoyed the symmetry of his heaps of ten coins and then he wanted them to form a square and then a larger square so that each coin "while it was itself a satisfaction bred a new desire." She also points out that he had been let down by human love and consolation and the money on the other hand, was reliable and seemed to stay with him.

> He began to think it was conscious of him as his loom was and he would on no account have exchanged those coins which had become his familiars for other coins with unknown faces.

She also shows understanding that money is the only thing that presented itself as something that a solitary man could own, control, and count (on). Other men have done similar things but their objects have been different: some erudite research project like that of the character Casaubon in George Eliot's novel Middlemarch (Eliot, 1874) or some special project which comes to stand as Marner's money did, for children and human love.

The circumstances for miserliness to develop are depicted by Eliot here as betrayal by human companions and a kind of exile. In addition to this she depicts an attack from the outside. Marner was given the quality of a "wise man" because he understood the power of herbs to help and cure, but of course there were many illnesses that he could not cure and his refusals to take on the role of saviour led to further rejection and an increased level of isolation from his neighbours. As a result he took out his money to admire it only when he could close his shutters and make fast his doors. Then he can run it through his fingers and see it shine in the darkness as his only light and guidance. The effect of this was to increase his isolation. He no longer roamed the hedgerows to gather the herbs that his mother had taught him to use and so he lost contact with nature as well as with his neighbours. In every way has life had shrunk and begun to flow in a single narrow channel.

Since miserliness has an effect, we expect that a spendthrift will have an impact on himself and on those around him. Eliot develops her theme of the power of money to demonstrate how much pain this causes. The local Squire has two sons, one of whom has made a foolish mistake in secretly marrying a loose woman enabling his younger brother to blackmail him. The younger brother, Dunstan, is motivated by greed and pride. Because he wants to get money at any emotional cost to his brother, he forces Godfrey to agree to sell his horse, Wildfire, Dunstan then wants to show off his riding on his brother's horse, so that he will cut a dashing figure and after he accidentally kills the horse through carelessness, his main regret is that he looks foolish walking home carrying his riding whip. The whip actually belongs to his brother but he has appropriated it because it has a gold handle.

All of this demonstrates the importance of wealth as status. Primogeniture led to strife between brothers but as we often see it still today, the main motivation for sibling destructiveness arises from the division of the parents' love which is symbolised by the division of the estate and of such good things as the golden handled whip and magnificent hunter. Dunstan robs Silas Marner of his precious gold because of this feeling of deprivation, although of course he has much more wealth than Marner. Here again, the love of money is shown in the Judeo- Christian light as the root of all evil. Eliot does much more than show the obsessionality of Marner's love for his money; she also shows the pathos of the man who has nothing more. The money is stolen and he becomes distraught. He desperately wants his money back and he accuses one of the villagers of stealing it but only because he must believe that someone local has taken it so that he can have some hope of being reunited with his money. Without it, he is bereaved.

Although the villagers do not know the extent of Marner's hoard, they are frightened and suspicious of him when he is so absorbed by it that he has no need of them, but when he loses it, they begin to soften towards him. Gifts of food were brought round and he was urged to attend church on Sunday or at least on Christmas Day to demonstrate that he was not receiving help or advice from the devil as some had suspected. Bad luck, especially in the form of losing money is likely to be more endearing to neighbours up to a point, than success and riches. Eliot makes very clear that the landed gentry were expected to provide generously from their wealth and that, at festivals like Christmas and New Year, there should be tables groaning with all the good things that the estate and the landowner's purse could provide. The Squire and the rich families are respected and well liked if they are generous and fair to their tenants but the poor humble weaver is respected only when he seems powerless and defeated. There is strong pressure for Marner to attend church which would symbolise his willingness to join the community and share its beliefs. In fact he does not go to church and seems not to understand the overtures of his neighbours as he is so unused to any kindness.

The main symbolic movement of the novel occurs when the disreputable cast-off wife of the Squire's son takes a drug and dies in the snow outside Marner's cottage. The golden-haired child, who is aged about two, wanders into the cottage out of the snow and lies down in front of the fire. Marner discovers her there and what he sees at first is gold. He thinks that his gold has returned because her golden curls are spread out on the hearth.

Marner is ready to transfer his attachment from the gold to the child although his emotions are not easily stirred. He refers to the child as "it" and clearly sees her arrival as replacement for his gold. Some of the possessiveness is transferred from the love of gold to the love of the child. When one of the neighbour women kindly tells him how to dress and look after the little child, he shows concern that she should still love him the best, not the woman who might seem more like a mother than he can be. There is perhaps some possessive control mixed in with the best of our love for children. The child's natural father feels the loss of her both as a gift that he could have given his childless wife and also as a loss of power that he would have had in bringing her up and Eliot describes his feeling on not having the courage to do more than ensure from a distance that she is safe.

The first thing that the child brings about for Marner is the kindness of his neighbour who urges him to have the child christened. He does this, and it brings him into the community. The child herself will not be loved and admired in secret behind closed doors like the gold but demands contact with the open air and the sun and above all with other people. Something of the idea of redemption appears in the way Eliot describes the effect of the child: "… for the little child had come to link him once more with the whole world." In addition, the coins that he earns for his weaving no longer have value in themselves. His hoard has gone and been completely replaced by the symbolic gold of the child.

There are few situations in which the value of gold is measured by its lack of equivalence to a human being, but there are plenty of therapeutic situations in which choices are made between human contacts and the greater reliability, as it is seen, of the accumulation of wealth. What Eliot shows so clearly is the fallacy of the trust in money and the pathology implied by the need to control and collect. Problems arise when controlling and collecting is a substitute for human contact or when it is the method of contact that is habitual.

Collecting of course takes the form not only of collecting money but also of collecting relationships. Most therapists will recognise the account of the man or woman who has serial or even co-existing relationships outside marriage or the acknowledged partnership.

> A successful business woman, Mrs A, is married with two young children. She is in her thirties, attractive and meets many men who seek to have a relationship with her. She has chosen to stay with her husband in spite of some difficulties in that relationship but she constantly reports new conquests. At first sight this could be seen as a form of collecting. What has emerged though is that the possibly anal urge to collect as many admirers as possible is linked to a more oral need for the unquestioning love of a mother which none of them can satisfy.

In social contexts, the need for this love is often expressed in serial relationships or in a ruthless quest for success which in our culture can be expressed in terms of money. Winning the National Lottery in the UK at present is to receive an anomalous prize. No doubt the person winning is ecstatic and thinks that all his troubles are over. The usual image that we have is of the winner spurting a stream of satisfying champagne all over himself and others. He then encounters the destructive power of envy and greed as well as a more obscure but equally powerful social disapproval of acquiring wealth with no effort. The conviction that money must be earned by honest toil may be less prevalent than it was in previous centuries, but it can surface in the face of what is seen as unreasonable wealth. The media use this to feed curiosity about how a person spends the money and journalists seek to satisfy the popular appetite to be assured that money does not bring happiness. Much of the press reporting assumes that interest is based on a common sense of schadenfreude, pleasure in another's distress. This is likely to impact any winner and together with whatever natural humanity they have, will lead to efforts to give away more or less judiciously, some of the money. Even this generosity may cause great ill feeling.

Poverty is a source of shame as Alice demonstrates when sent to a school that her parents could not really afford. Charles Dickens wrote of the devastating effect of debt on Victorian society in Little Dorrit (Dickens, 1857) and shows how the inmates, as a result of imprisonment in the Marshalsea debtor's prison, were treated like children which led to their behaving like children. Shakespeare, on the other hand, wrote of the power of money in opposition to the power of love in 'The Merchant of Venice' (1598). The suitors are set the task of choosing between three caskets: lead, silver, and gold to win the lady. Those who choose on the basis of the value of the metals lose. The hero, Bassanio, chooses the lead casket because he sees gold as gaudy and silver as the "common drudge twixt man and man" but lead is honest and promises no more than it delivers. He is right and is worthy of the lady.

Abuse and cruelty are poured upon the Jews while the Christians, with or without money, see themselves as inherently superior. Money went also with beauty:

> In Belmont is a lady richly left
> And she is fair, and fairer than that word
> Of wondrous virtues. (Act I, Scene i)

Shylock hates the Christians not only because they are Christians but also because they lend out money free of interest and bring down the rate of interest in Venice. Yet they are also carrying out business and Antonio expects great rewards from his ships that are to bring back profit from overseas. When his daughter elopes with Lorenzo who is a Christian and takes all his gold, Shylock is mocked for being equally distressed by both losses, confusing money with love:

> My daughter! O my ducats! O my daughter,
> Fled with a Christian! O my Christian ducats! (Act II, Scene viii)

But money is not everything to him. When Antonio fails to repay because his ships have miscarried, Shylock will not take the money, even when he is offered more than his bond. He wants revenge. This is clearly one of the themes of the play but the confusion of money and relationship is also clear. The "pound of flesh" of the bond is in itself a symbol of that confusion. Gerard (2000) points out that Portia's first question is about identity and relationship: "Which is the merchant here and which the Jew?" (Act IV, Scene i), as though it would be difficult to distinguish between them.

Alice brings a view of the social position that money conveys when she describes the house that she lived in and the effect on the local children of her attending a private school. Her parents were struggling to pay for the house and for her school but they had acquired the values that led them to try to do this from educated or aspiring parents of their own. This is not to say of course that working-class people were unable or even unlikely to share these aspirations. What Alice reports is seeing that in practice, she was caught between the snobbery of the well off and the anger and envy of the less well off. Her parents managed to get her to university and the provision of the 1944 Education Act in England meant that she could have her fees paid by means of a State Scholarship. Lack of money might well have prevented this and left her bored and unfulfilled in a menial job. Both Alice's grandmother and mother-in-law demonstrate the suffering of bright and potentially powerful women denied education and a job that would use their potential. Their pride is injured by the need to be supported by their husbands and they constantly seek ways to rule over a domain of some sort however small.

Money or the lack of it determines position in society as well as the comfort or ease of the life lived there. Social class is a powerful predictor of educational attainment as well as health and life expectancy. Social distinctions are based on birth, education, and related to these are the divisions created by the possession of money. Alice demonstrates that this position can be changed but for the first generation the change is not made without difficulty and some humiliation. Money has the power to change the people that an individual can meet and the occupations that he can choose.

CHAPTER TEN

Who pays for psychotherapy?

Economic transactions function because I want something which another person possesses and which they will transfer to me if I offer something desirable in return. Whether we like it or not there is a market in psychotherapy, counselling, and psychoanalysis. Because of the vast pit of mental suffering and despair in the community, the services of these professionals are needed. Often these services are needed by those who cannot work or who cannot find the work that they are ready and willing to do and therefore cannot pay for what they need. The usual rules of the market cannot be left to match supply and demand or the most vulnerable will be left without help. There is another area in which this rule does work. This is of course the private psychological therapy offered to those who can afford to pay. As long as there are enough of those people, there will be a supply of trained therapists who can also provide some services through charities and organisations that do not pay them much if anything.

While this small pool of private work is crucial, it will depend greatly on the narratives that any given society currently believes about the nature and value of psychological therapy. Writers like Professor Frank Furedi of the University of Kent provide a narrative of scepticism. Furedi promotes an idea of the "counselling industry" in which he argues against any idea of "vulnerable" or "damaged" people being helped by experts. On the University of Kent website he writes:

> Alongside my study of risk consciousness, I have explored the cultural influences that have encouraged society to become risk-averse and to feel a heightened sense of vulnerability. The defining feature of people is increasingly represented as their vulnerability and it is frequently suggested we live in an age where people's mental health and emotions are permanently under siege. (Furedi, 2011)

In his book, Therapy Culture, Furedi (2003) attacks the "industry" and one aspect of the implied criticism is that people make money from an objective and mass produced approach to individual suffering. On the other hand he is against recognition of suffering at all as this creates victims and separates out those who can help.

Rustin (2001, p. 176) pointed out that it seems faintly wrong to be talking about money and cost in the context of one of the most personal and intimate forms of therapy that there can be. Love is the subject of therapy although the interaction is paid for in the common medium of exchange of the market place. Nevertheless, therapists have to live and if they are to train for six or seven years, invest in expensive personal therapy and continuing supervision as many do, they will need to earn a living.

In this environment, how is psychotherapy to be funded? What are the effects of private, NHS or third-sector funding: what are the political implications of different funding sources and most importantly, what are the clinical implications? This chapter will consider the funding prospects for our work and the arguments that have taken place and need to take place about our work and state or insurance funding that may be tied to state regulation and guidelines and requirements.

If the payment of fees for psychoanalysis is important, as this book has argued, then the question of where the money comes from is crucial. No less important is the question of who owns psychoanalysis and therefore is the rightful recipient of these fees. In a 2004 book on the ownership of psychoanalysis, Darien Leader wrote of the unique situation in Britain by which the ownership of psychoanalysis is claimed by the British Psycho-analytic Society. "Psychoanalysis is a field of enquiry and a set of therapeutic practices. It is not a unified body of knowledge or a unified practice but a movement with multiple traditions" (2004, p. 256). He makes this point to support the argument that no one school can claim to train all psychoanalysts in the country, which is the claim of the British Psycho-analytic Society. This has not always been accepted meekly but on the whole, psychoanalytic psychothera-pists and psychoanalysts trained in a different way have allowed this hegemony to continue.

Does this affect the financial balance of the profession? The answer to this question is variable at different times and according to different groups. The UK Government in 2011 stepped back from statutory regu-lation of the professions of psychoanalysis, psychotherapy, and counsel-ling leaving the ownership of the field to the professionals themselves and to the public who may or may not accept what the professionals say to them.

This is perhaps the best scenario to allow psychoanalysis and its derivative therapies to flourish. Rules are proposed but on the whole flouted. Those who wish to accept the rules can do so but there is no punishment for those who do not. Professional ethics of course do pro-vide rules and sanctions that are followed by professional societies. This contrasts with the situation in countries which have chosen to legislate the provision of analytic therapy, limiting it, for example, to those who hold a degree in medicine or psychology as in Italy. Michael Rustin wrote of his experience of psychoanalysts in the Czech Republic where the Communist regime had been hostile to private discussion of thoughts and ideas and only vestigial practice continued by those who were brave enough to risk being reported to the authorities for subversive activities. Rustin points out that essential conditions for psychoanalysis to flourish include a toleration of private practice, pri-vate conversations, and private contracts for the delivery of services (2001, p. 164). Rustin goes on to outline the history of psychoanalysis as a profession with some important allies such as the National Health Service in Britain but also many disadvantages. He concludes that only through people hearing of the benefits of psychoanalysis by word of mouth usually, and seeking out their own treatment and then handing over a fee to the therapist could this fragile and private process survive (2001, p. 169).

Rustin also makes the point that a society needs to have a vigorous literary and academic life where books and journals are freely available in the market so that people can read the works of Freud and his more modern interpreters.

Rustin recognises that if we advocate the private contract of psychoanalysis we are also advocating unequal access. Not everyone in a capitalist society can afford psychoanalysis. Should we not therefore wish for it to be part of the state provision for those who are in need? State involvement means state control to at least some extent. Anthony Molino described what happened when in 1989 Italy passed a law to regulate the profession of psychotherapy. This is known as Law 56: Any and all practitioners of any model of psychotherapy must hold a degree in medicine or psychology. This is of course rigorously defended by the practitioners who are limiting their field but is also contested on various grounds by those who are on the outside. Molino (2001) quotes Cesare Viviano who writes that the field of psychotherapy has become an industry where the subjective relationship is

> subject to [the] intrusive management … and insurance bureaucra-
> cies interested more in diagnostic categories and per capita session
> revenue than the experiential fruits of psychoanalysis. (2001, p. 185)

These lines show the general attitude of those who resist state regulation and licensing of analytic practice. The whole is more than the sum of the parts. It also shows the combination of regulation as a form of codification with financial interest in income and taxation. One of the most important elements of regulation for some therapists has been the potential expense for the therapists and the income for the state or a state run authority. This income whether or not hypothecated would be seen as contributing to sustain a bureaucracy that would seek an ever increasing level of control over the process of psychotherapy.

The quotation also mentions the "insurance bureaucracies" and reminds us that the alternative to state funding of psychoanalysis through an agency like the National Health Service (NHS) in the UK is a form of funding through insurance. From the patient's point of view, having therapy funded through either of these methods is similar. He pays a sum, compulsorily in the case of the NHS, and when he needs therapy he is given it because he has already paid for it. The difficulty in both cases is that you do not choose your therapy or your therapist. Within the NHS you are allocated therapy as the result of a brief triage session with a General Practitioner who will assess your level or depression of anxiety using a standard inventory of questions. This will result in a referral for further therapy according to a stepped care hierarchy mostly providing Cognitive Behavioural Therapy and now mostly drawn from one of the therapies approved by the National Institute for Clinical Excellence. This will usually be a form of brief therapy that is very often helpful at the time but needs more evidence for long-term effectiveness.

Would Alice have been well served by this form of therapy provided in the UK by her GP? She might have been suffering from mild depression at the beginning and would have been offered the first step of the stepped care that was approved by the National Institute for Clinical Excellence (NICE). This would have meant examining her thought processes in a much more active way than her psychoanalytic therapist, Margaret, does. She might have been less frustrated and would have been guided to go home and complete cognitive tasks to correct faulty ways of thinking. Of course this is what psychoanalytic therapy does over time. Alice is able to change her anger and frustration into something much more constructive by the end of this account but she does have to make major changes in her life and work. No-one can know whether she would have been able to do this in short-term cognitive work but what we can say is that she has a chance for this change to last because she arrived at it herself through a long-term process of evolution and development with the hand of the therapist lightly touching her arm every now and then (metaphorically).

Alice seems to benefit from bringing together the threads of her own story which is then heard both by her therapist and by her own conscious and unconscious mind. She also benefits from the intensity of listening that her therapist gives her. This sort of intensive listening deserves consideration. It is one of the first things that is taught in counselling courses but is none the less a major skill that can be learned in time, but experience shows that some people are better disposed to listen than others. Attentive listening may involve an open mind that has no clear plan for the speaker but simply registers what is being said. This sort of listening was perhaps intended by Wilfred Bion in his famous aphorism that the therapist should be without memory and without desire. He says that memory and desire can be the false idols that distracts the patient from recognition of whoever or whatever his god might be (1967, p. 145). The mother provides this open reverie in her preoccupation with her infant and while she may or may not speak about the fear that the infant shows her, she contains it by her continued presence and her ability to accept the infant's disturbance without getting too disturbed herself. Listening without rushing to provide the cure for which the patient thinks he is paying requires experience and faith in the value of the analytic experience.

So far, there is little evidence that states do run or are able to run the kind of psychotherapy that allows for people who are not mentally ill but whose lives are not worth living through various patterns and beliefs that could be examined and perhaps changed in the course of analytic work. In the UK, the State can and does concern itself with mental illness and more recently with mild-to-moderate depression and anxiety which has been shown to cost the community many days of lost work. Lord Richard Layard's report on Depression published in 2006 brings together economics and finance in his clear rationale for providing better access to psychological therapies. His rationale was the financially based one that the whole society would benefit if we could improve the depression and anxiety that so many people (he estimates one in six of the population) either does suffer or will at some point in their lives. Mental illness accounts for 40% of absence from work and takes up "at least a third of GP time" (Layard, 2006, p. 3). Layard claimed that we could treat this great pit of depression if we would be willing for the State to spend the money on our behalf to treat it. He says that at the time the cost of providing computerised CBT for each person suffering mild-to-moderate depression would be only £750.

> But can we afford the £750 it costs to treat someone? The money which the government spends will pay for itself. For someone on Incapacity Benefit costs us £750 a month in extra benefits and lost taxes. If the person works just a month more as a result of the treatment, the treatment pays for itself. (2006, p. 2)

All forms of therapy can of course claim that they are benefitting society by helping people to address depression that keeps them from getting up in the morning and contributing in any way. Because Layard is seeking here to persuade the British Government to undertake this treatment on a vast, national scale, he is also emphasising the evidence base. It would be surprising if he were to expect large sums to be put into therapies that cannot demonstrate satisfactory outcomes. There has been and still is some debate about what constitutes an evidence base and which therapies can show that they have one.

This report is clear and emphatic and has had great influence on the psychological therapies in the UK. It has forced all the other modalities that are not stamped with his seal of approval to find their own clients and to demonstrate their efficacy and effectiveness.

This interest in the talking therapies has led to setting up various committees such as the National Mental Health Development Unit (NHDU) in times of plenty when money could be found to improve policy and services in the UK. However, as money from government sources dries up in times of financial stringency, the future even of the provision of such therapies as short-term Cognitive Behaviour Therapy is thrown into doubt and the NHDU is to be disbanded after only two years. Even when the Government of the time seems to support the view that the early experience of an individual affects the present mental functioning, professionals might be reluctant to support a programme. Ian McPherson writes:

> The end result may not be what the sector wishes to see and its reputation could be tarnished by association with an increasingly politicised debate about how to progress mental health policy implementation in a system going through massive reconfiguration in a financially challenged environment. (2011)

McPherson emphasises that there is a gap between government initiatives and the trust of the professionals who will not simply take the money and run. They want to know that the programme with which they are engaging is professionally sound rather than simply offering much needed money in the short term. Nevertheless, if clinicians refuse to get involved with initiatives, they run the risk that the analytic model will be side-lined and will receive no funding for potential impoverished patients or for research and development. There may be many who do not want anything to do with such funding but they might not be happy if funding continues to go to those practising other models.

McPherson is also pointing to the general trend to appoint non clinicians to act as Chief Executives to professional bodies where the need is seen to be for a business person rather than someone who understands the clinic. Such backgrounds enable them to deal with the financial climate but may lead to difficulties in understanding the anxieties of the clinicians. Running a psychotherapy organisation of any sort costs money and the money comes either from the members of the organisation or from the clients or from charities and state or voluntary sources. Whatever the source, such organisations running clinics are likely to be affected by the ups and downs of a given economy. While patients are a priority and will usually be well cared for, those therapists reliant on government funding will be expected to see clients for the shortest possible time and to close cases after only a few sessions when longer- term therapy might have had a better outcome.

In 1986, Howard, Kopta, Krauss, and Orlinsky carried out research reported by Freedman, Hoffenberg, Vorus, and Frosch (1999) to determine the optimal "dosage" for patients. He had found that the maximum effect was achieved in up to twenty-eight sessions with diminishing returns after that point. Later research from the same research group put it at fifty-six sessions and this improvement was maintained in the subjects for two and four years after termination. They found significant differences between patients staying in treatment for six to twelve months and those who stayed for twelve to twenty-four months and also over twenty-five months. Longer-term patients showed improved functioning according to the measures used in the study. (Freedman, Hoffenberg, Vorus, and Frosch,1999, p. 742). This has obvious cost implications for clients. The subjects in the study (99 of them) were all attending the IPTAR Clinical Centre in the United States, which is a low-cost clinic where clients pay their own fees, mostly without assistance from outside bodies. We may note that 55% of the clients were attending one session a week, 32% two and 8% three. This of course will have an impact on the effect of the therapy and on its accessibility for the majority of potential clients.

If it were possible to demonstrate the effectiveness of high-intensity therapy and that it is more effective than therapy at lower levels, we would have to acknowledge that this is a benefit that is denied to the majority of people on low incomes. Berghout, Zevalkink, and Hakkaart-van Roijen (2010) published one of the few studies of the cost benefits of long-term psychoanalysis, contrasted not with short-term work but with three times weekly psychoanalytic psychotherapy. Psychoanalysis was more costly than psychoanalytic psychotherapy, but also more effective from a health-related quality of life perspective. Quality-adjusted life-years (QALYs) were estimated for each treatment strategy using the SF-6D. Total costs were calculated from a societal perspective (treatment costs plus other societal costs) and discounted at 4%. The incremental cost-effectiveness ratio (ICER)— that is, the extra costs to gain one additional QALY by delivering psychoanalysis instead of psychoanalytic psychotherapy—was estimated at 52,384 per QALY gained. Psychoanalysis was more costly than psychoanalytic psychotherapy, but also more effective from a health-related quality of life perspective. From the summary published on-line in 2010 it is difficult to assess the extra benefit gained from the intensive psychoanalysis but the numbers in the study were substantial, at about 200, and the study should be useful. Older studies have shown that outpatient psychotherapy reduced the amount of inpatient treatment for physical disease that was needed. The study by Berghout, Zevalkink, and Hakkaart-van Roijen certainly emphasises that apart from the Depression Report there are few cost-benefit analyses published. Some private practice therapists would not wish to be involved in such a study but many worry about the value of their work, especially when they are unclear about how much benefit a client is obtaining from the process.

Insurance

Many companies now offer packages to their senior staff that include health insurance. Someone who has health insurance whether paid for privately or by an employer is likely to expect that psychotherapy would be funded by the insurer. In its web-based therapist finder service, the Chicago Association for Psychoanalytic Psychology (2011) points out that "the frequency of sessions covered by most insurance plans is once a week or less and usually the patient must pay for some portion of the cost out of pocket." They also point out that some insurers will refuse to use all the therapists who are qualified. They are concerned that this model of therapy opens it to undue interference by insurers, whose interest might be financial, with what is offered and tends towards a medical model overseen by psychiatrists who are bound to be taken as the authorities. In the UK, the main company offering insurance registers therapists itself and has views on the modality of therapy that will be acceptable. It and will not allow any therapists not registered with it to offer funded therapy.

Other sources of funded therapy are the employee assistance programmes (EAP's). These offer therapy that is funded by employers when psychological problems are seen to be interfering with performance. Some employers are concerned with well-being and will send their employees for therapy to help with problems that could be categorised as dis-ease rather than disease and before they are interfering grossly with performance. Whatever the need and the reason for offering therapy, what is offered is likely to be short term, usually only six sessions. A moral question arises when therapists have to decide whether or not to offer ongoing private practice sessions to those who have formed an attachment as they come to the end of their six funded sessions.

Some patients have brought elements of the payment method to the therapy and thus opened the possibility of analysing what it means. Abramson (2001) quotes the American analyst Joseph Slap, who describes the payment process for a patient who was being funded both by insurers and by a sum of money from a tax refund:

> Initially, I assumed that the patient was expressing in oral terms her feeling of being phallically deprived. However, the men in the manifest dreams were without a trace of erotism or aggressiveness, unlike those who had previously served in her dreams and fantasies as phallic suppliers. (John Kennedy and John Wayne had been prototypes.) I concluded that the material of the analysis had shifted to an oral level. It seemed to me that while the greater part of the patient's analytic expense was covered by insurance and tax refunds she felt like an infant for whom everything is provided with nothing asked for in exchange. (Slap, 1976)

Abramson (2001) goes on:

> This article is a case report of the psychoanalytic treatment of a severely disturbed patient who had multiple self-injurious episodes and who has psychotic ideas. The frequency of sessions and duration of the treatment has been 4 days-a-week for 8 years. During this time, the treatment has taken place in the context of a treatment team from the state department of mental health whose role has been to provide the supportive framework that allowed the patient to survive. The team and therapist have met once a month, with the patient present, to discuss progress and problems in management. Before the initiation of her therapy, the patient had had multiple hospitalizations because of suicidal ideation and self-injurious behaviour. One and a half years after her therapy was initiated, and concurrent with the establishment of a strong transference to her therapist, the frequency and length of hospitalizations declined markedly. In spite of the high frequency of sessions and long

duration of the treatment, the still ongoing cost of psychoanalytic
treatment has been less than would have been repeated hospitaliza-
tions. In addition, the life of this patient has been saved, and there
is a real possibility that she will be able to recover the ability to live
an emotionally productive life. (2001, pp. 253–254).

This is an unusual situation in that the patient was open to examining
the funding sources of her therapy. In the case of most people attending
an Employee Assistance Programme, there is little time in the six sessions usually provided for considering this aspect of the work. Many
people who use this facility are angry with their employers and regard
them as a source of their problems and would be likely to think that the
employer should pay. This would be seen as the least that they can do.
This level of anger might be brought down by the end of the therapy as
the patient becomes more able to feel his own sense of power and value
returning. In some cases this will lead to a willingness to fund sessions
of his own after the funded sessions and even though the same therapist is not usually permitted to continue, such people will be able to
seek therapy in due course because they have had a good experience.

   Short-term therapy has increasingly invaded the areas of funded
therapy but it has not completely replaced long-term work. Adolf
Grunbaum wrote in 1986:

> As we know, classical long term psychoanalytic treatment has fallen
> on hard times in the USA.

But

> so called psychoanalytically oriented psychotherapy of shorter
> duration still needs to be reckoned with in this country.
> (1986, p. 263)

He added that he ventured to think that psychoanalytic ideas still held
an important place in various forms of therapy that do not necessarily
acknowledge their debt to Freud.

   Elisabeth Roudinesco, a Lacanian psychoanalyst, writes of psychoanalysis as a discipline that cannot be tied down to ownership.

> As a discipline psychoanalysis belongs to no-one. To no state, to no
> country, to no institution. And while professional societies appear

to wish to represent it exclusively, for the most part it overflows
from the framework that attempts to constrain it. (2004, p. 178)

Organisations or even states may claim psychoanalysis by paying for
its practice but the discipline itself will always question the very con-
straints that seek to limit it. Ideas cannot be owned in spite of copy
right and rights over intellectual property that may be conveyed by the
law. Fortunately for the rest of us, Freud's ideas did not stay frozen like
bees in amber but have continued to develop and change with the passage of time and with the experience of each new generation. Robert
Hinshelwood points out that ideas are not equal to money (1994, p. 43).
They may circulate but they do not stay with the next possessor. Once
put out into the world, they cannot be possessed however much Freud
himself wished to control the future of his theories.

By and large, companies, governments, and statutory organisations
have been kept from any intrusion into the privacy of the psychoanalytic process even when they are funding it. Bollas and Sundelson
(1995) wrote of the principle of confidentiality and the danger they perceived from intrusions from the State. They quoted Dr Joseph Lifshutz
in California who was imprisoned briefly for refusing to testify about
a former patient even though the patient had made his own therapy
known (1995, pp. 13–14). The important consequence of this case was
the affirmation that psychotherapists do not have absolute privilege in
law in California. The extent of privilege is to be decided case by case.
This decision is not widely known in the UK and probably does not
concern patients in the rest of the world unduly but it does at least leave
the possibility that the public interest will not prevail over the individual interest in all circumstances.

This question of legal privilege relates to the question of ownership
and although the position is not yet clear at the time of writing, it is still
at least possible that psychoanalysis belongs to the patient and the therapist and is not to be hijacked even in the public interest. This is a very
important point because it promotes the proposition that psychological
therapy is for the individual, not for society as a whole. This might lead
us back to the view that the individual should pay for it even though we
know that this limits access and bases the use of the service on money
and wealth. Paradoxically, following from this, psychological therapy
can assert its awkward and often inconvenient demand that the individual should be respected no matter how much money he has.

PART III

WHAT MONEY SAYS TO THERAPISTS

CHAPTER ELEVEN

How money talks to therapists

Psychoanalytic theorists have faced some of the primary and most difficult questions about the nature of human beings. They therefore try to identify the psychological imperatives that we need to consider in understanding what goes on in the human mind. In the mid twentieth century, the psychoanalyst W. R. D. Fairbairn based a complex theoretical structure on his answer to the philosophical problem of the nature of desire:

> Libido is not primarily pleasure seeking but object seeking. (1946, p. 137)

This was a revolutionary idea as philosophers in the eighteenth and nineteenth centuries had generally postulated that human beings seek pleasure and avoid pain as their primary motivation. Freud (1920) had accepted that hypothesis as a basis for his thought, particularly in the process by which we defend against painful thoughts and resist moving from being governed by the pleasure principle to the reality principle (1920).

Fairbairn made another contribution to thinking about psychic structure: he added the possibility of an exciting object to the dynamics that are possible in the unconscious. The relationship with an object may be primarily connected with one of the zones of the body (oral, anal, or genital) that Freud associated with developmental stages. If we associate the interest in money with the stage of developing control, we can understand the tension that is involved in making sure that there is no mess visible, partly because there would be relief in evacuating the contents of the bowels. Just as there is a reward of approval for holding on to faeces, there can be pleasure that may be associated with all the activities connected with accumulating and spending money for its own sake. Like the pleasure connected with the bowels, this pleasure is not socially approved.

People come to see analytic therapists for all sorts of reasons but generally they are seeking a clearer sense of identity and both the ability to be separate and the ability to relate to others. Because of this need, the medium of exchange between people is of vital importance. Analytic therapists meet anxieties in their patients related to all forms of exchange. Money is only one of these. Such anxieties, both conscious and unconscious are widely known and understood in the prevailing western culture. Because the patient must pay the therapist for therapy that is delivered in private practice, conscious anxieties will surface about the cost and length of therapy. Some of these have been discussed above. Anxieties about deeply buried fears are more difficult to address and the therapist has to find ways of coming to understand these and then conveying them to the patient so that the conscious mind can grapple with what they mean.

This book has considered greed, and the defences against it, debt and its concomitant shame and guilt. In the story of Alice, we also see the difficulty caused by theft. This is a component of guilt even when there is no question of an actual theft taking place. This chapter will consider how the therapist recognises and works with these. Power and its lack are also important for the patient and the therapist will see how money provides a matrix for understanding the patient's position more clearly. If money is not discussed because of diffidence or shame on the part of the therapist, the effect on the patient may be discovered. One possibility is that the patient perceives the therapist as lacking in power or lacking in confidence in her power. This might for some patients be equivalent to seeing the mother without phallic power. At a deep level this can lead to anxiety for both women and men because they have to grapple with the possible loss of their own power.

Therapists deal with debt and with the guilt that arises from a sense of having taken something from someone. Ownership implies theft. Sitting in her consulting room, the therapist seems to shut out the external world, creating a warm, comfortable space with two people, no-one else. Yet each of the two participants is embedded in a social context. As emphasised by the American psychoanalyst, Fromm (1942), the individual functions in a context. Like Winnicott (1953), he emphasised that understanding the individual requires a consideration of the social background that makes him what he is.

In 1951 the British psychiatrist and psychoanalyst Donald Winnicott (paper first published in 1953) conceived the transitional object in a way that helps us to see that the state of mind of the infant who is often deprived of the feeding breast or bottle and of his excreta is in need of a way of conceptualising what is his and is in his power and what is other and outside his control. The object that is held and cherished by the infant, maybe a piece of cloth or a favourite stuffed animal, has the quality of being external and yet being imbued with meaning by the infant and so in a sense is part of the infant. Winnicott's concept helps us understand what is going on in the mind of a thief.

Property and Theft

Gedo (1963) suggested that, for a thief, stolen goods function as a transitional object. They are at once both him and not him. Winnicott (1953) wrote:

> Thieving can be described in terms of an individual's unconscious urge to bridge a gap in continuity of experience in respect of a transitional object. (1953, p. 97)

A good mother allows the infant to feel that he possesses her breast and only gradually disillusions him, introducing the separation brought about by the idea of property.

In the consulting room we often hear stories of betrayal and consequent inability to trust:

> Mr L has just ended a relationship with his gay partner after three years. He discovered that his partner was going out to gay bars and was actively seeking sex through gay websites. This for him

constituted a betrayal since he had thought that they would enter a Civil Partnership and stay together. He was finding it difficult to concentrate on his work and even more difficult to make friends with other men, especially if they were gay. He was offered a promotion at this time and tried to console himself with the idea that he would be better off on his own both emotionally and financially. This was not an adequate source of comfort that he was able to use and he began to access the gay dating sites on the internet with the specific intention of finding one-off sexual partners. He was ashamed of his own response but was able to see that he was, among other things, shoring up his own sense of value in the terms that his ex-partner had demonstrated to him.

This need to demonstrate value can translate into the wish to be seen to be generous, both to others and to the therapist. Alice becomes anxious that if she is not paying as much as others, she will not be liked and cared for well enough. If Margaret encouraged it, she would find herself offering to pay more and possibly more than she could afford in order to equal or outdo the others, even though she does not know the others or what they are actually paying. This leads to the rivalry and jealousy of the socially expressed Oedipus complex. The intrigues of the wish to be the only love of the parent of the opposite sex are played out in every office and board room. They are not restricted to the opposite sex but are very often seen among groups of the same sex such as groups of mothers at a play-group or men at a pub. A natural leader often emerges and then the other members begin to arrange which of them will be the favourite lieutenant. The result may be the family scenario for each person played out in the social context.

Mrs B had three brothers and her father appeared only interested in them. Her efforts to collect other men seemed to be an attempt to bring those brothers under control while at the same time finding the one who will be able to make her feel that she has won her father's interest and approval at last. Noticeable in her case is that her own success and income seem poor consolations for not having the father's love. She sends him money as he is widowed and lonely but this does not have the desired effect. Her money seems useless to her if it does not work in this context.

Power

The moment when a patient enters the room is the moment when power is in question. Simple matters like the question of who sits where are indicators for the patient. Some people begin by hanging back and waiting to be shown which chair to choose. Others barge in and choose the therapist's chair. This is awkward but is usually best dealt with straight away. Therapists have recounted sitting in the wrong chair because they couldn't bring themselves to say that they wanted the patient to change. However the therapist deals with it, the opportunity arises to examine how it might feel to be in the therapist's chair rather than the patient's.

Most people will leave the therapist to speak first as a sign of deference to the fact that this is her territory. Human beings behave like other animals to the extent that they seek to know what the parameters of any relationship are going to be and to locate themselves in that relationship at the fundamental level of gender, which we notice and identify about a stranger before anything else, except perhaps race. Many elements of history and cultural background will be immediately in play. Since money is one of the counters which must be negotiated in the relationship, it will be part of this early exploration.

The patient's wish to control

Because in order to control the bowels a child must learn to control the muscles of excretion, Freud saw a mental correlate in the desire and need for control at all levels. The obsessional aspect of character derives therefore from the part of the mind that wants and needs control. Collecting is one obvious manifestation of control. "These stamps are all mine and I arrange them as I wish." Collecting coins is an acceptable hobby while collecting money is less admired although in practice it is much more common than philately. Alice has plenty of money at the beginning and there is a rational explanation for her reluctance to part with money but she is also inclined to want to hold on to what she has for psychological reasons as much as for practical necessity.

Some aspects of obsessionality can be seen in the sudden anxiety that Alice feels about the room, the chairs, and the couch: Who has been there before? Freud looks at this anxiety about cleanliness and hygiene as a derivative from the small child's enjoyment of dirt.

He cites the willingness of the toddler to play with his own faeces and to enjoy smearing and making a mess with paint, food, and anything else that is wet and of a similar consistency. The adult learns of course that this sort of behaviour is not acceptable and represses it to the extent that many people have difficulty in freeing themselves up enough to paint, use clay, or even cook. He links exaggerated anxiety in this area to a wish to revert to the messiness of childhood that is being repressed but is threatening to return to consciousness. Nevertheless, there is a rational component to the need for hygiene. Every winter we have viruses that spread through lack of care. Washing hands before eating seems a sensible thing to do. The threat of a flu pandemic is with us each year and there is serious reason to seek to avoid whatever we are told is the current dangerous virus.

When this anxiety interferes with ordinary living, for example, preventing someone from using public transport, it is pathological and needs to be extinguished. Analytic work can help to understand the hidden wish and can give more freedom in the choice of behaviour but Cognitive Behaviour Therapy has success in the immediate transformation of the behaviour. Cognitive therapists will seek to find the specific fears that are being denied with the obsessional behaviour. Behavioural work can then extinguish the fears through exposure to them. The skill of the therapist will lie in the process by which the exposure to the fears is measured and managed. The analytic therapist will be equally interested in the underlying fears and will use the analytic techniques to help towards a greater understanding of the deep-seated reasons for defences and for the meaning conveyed by the specific defences chosen. Analytic work will take longer but might well enable people to find what is hidden deep down in the seams and ribs of the geology of their minds.

Getting into debt

Patients deal differently with the sense that they owe the therapist a symbolic debt. The more she helps, the more the pain of debt might be. Since this sense of debt is inevitable if she is useful, it can be made into a useful and constructive medium for understanding what troubles the patient. When a patient cannot bear much help, the sense of debt and the guilt that it brings will need to be examined in relation to its source.

Some kinds of debt have roots in giving. The unfaithful partner, whose actions form so many narratives, gives something of him or herself away and this gift creates a debt to the original partner. Debts created by unfaithfulness are both monetary and emotional. The marital home may have to be sold if the partnership breaks under the strain. Children will have to be supported often at the most expensive time of their lives. Marriage settlements were the vehicle by which fathers ensured that their daughters would not be left penniless by a feckless or unfaithful husband. Now prenuptial agreements are often required by the rich to ensure a fair distribution of wealth if a relationship breaks down.

Of course each person will have a different debt. Alice expected to be told that she must pay a standard fee to the psychotherapist and is very much alarmed at the idea that she will have to make up her own mind about how much she wants to give. She is then even more alarmed to be given the gift of a low fee by her therapist. She is immediately on her guard about what might be wanted in return. Freud points out to us that there is a deeper layer to this concern. Alice is reminded of a father who was not always firm and clear in his demands and she is frightened by the apparent weakness of the therapist. She is likely to have somewhere deep in her unconscious the female wish for phallic power. In that sense she does wish to have what the man has. She wants control or "the maistrie" as Chaucer's Wife of Bath puts it in her answer to the question "What does the woman want?"

In thinking about Alice's attitude to the setting of a fee, we can find some further insights from the work of Melanie Klein in the twentieth century. Because the child of either sex is affected by envy of the adults of both sexes, envy has an impact on the developing attitude to acquiring money, saving it, and spending it. Klein developed analytic ideas in a consideration of the child's fantasies about the body of the mother (1959). Many of these are unconscious and therefore will be known as phantasies. She points out that the child is afraid of his father's anger which might lead to castration but both the girl and the boy envy the mother's ability to bear children. They think of the mother's body as the place where the baby and also therefore the father's penis are located. In phantasy, the child attacks and destroys the mother's possessions (Klein, 1959). We need not be surprised that the child at this stage wants to acquire his or her own goods. Envy leads to a need to amass possessions. We know about the battles that take place in nursery schools over the possession of a particular crayon or set of bricks. If what is demanded is not in fact only the crayon but also what it symbolises, no amount of offering another equally good crayon will help. The point is to have what the other child has and once getting it, to hang on to it. Alice demonstrates anxiety about hanging on to what she has. What she would not yet be able to put into words would be her underlying envy of the therapist who is already in the place of mother and therefore will be susceptible to the envy that Klein describes.

Destructiveness

Envy can be destructive. Freud discusses both destructiveness and guilt in Civilisation and its Discontents (1930). Repressing guilt may cause social problems such as scapegoating. One of the main themes of psychoanalysis is that much human behaviour is brought about by unconscious defences against pain. Mental pain is involved in the honest acceptance of our worst impulses and the human mind therefore seeks to avoid this recognition through defences leading to repression. The love of money is one of the motives for the primary mythical crime in which brothers unite to kill the father and take his place, his power and his possessions. Freud distinguishes between the remorse that can be felt for an act that has been committed and the primal guilt for the crime that we want to commit but did not actually carry out.

This phenomenon is helpful in understanding much clinical work, particularly, though not exclusively with men. In George Eliot's Silas Marner the Squire's two sons play out the greed of sons in taking some of the wealth from the father. The elder son is presented as more responsible and kinder. He gives his father's money to his feckless younger brother and then he suffers both remorse and guilt. Godfrey's plight reminds us of the importance of debt as a social phenomenon. He is being blackmailed by his younger brother because of his marriage which Eliot herself seems to disapprove because of the social and financial disparity between the couple. In this she was expressing the social norm of her time. It was bound to end badly, she seems to be telling us.

The moral judgments of a novelist are made clearer than those of a therapist but that does not mean that a therapist can avoid making them. The therapist who might well disapprove of a liaison for her own reasons seeks to keep her disapproval to herself until she can make constructive use of it. An illustration of constructive use might be found if you imagine working with Godfrey as a patient. He needs to hear his generosity affirmed and at the same time his lust for the attractive girl would need to be recognised and accepted. He seems to want to expunge his sin by dong the honourable thing and marrying the girl. The question for the therapist to explore with him might be whether he could marry the woman who is pregnant without being ashamed of her and feeling that he must hide her. Does she in fact represent his sin? If he could be brought to think about this aspect of his action, he might have a choice over proceeding.

Godfrey is a debtor because of both weakness and strength. He is weak to give in to his impulses which society forbids but he is generous only in giving in his own way. He is rendered powerless by the debt that he cannot repay and which he simply has to own with bowed head. His father is understandably angry and Godfrey feels profoundly humiliated because he loves his father and appreciates his generosity. This makes him depressed and angry, both the result of frustration and impotence. He suffers both shame and guilt although his primary experience is guilt over what he has done.

Debt and its defences

Debt in general leads to a sense of impotence and a restriction of power which is likely to lead to depression. At the other end of the spectrum, debt can encourage a manic form of denial in which the patient can go on adding debt to debt. The American psychoanalyst, Bass (2007), writes of a patient he calls Helena, who demonstrated the social expression of debt:

> To be in debt to me would constitute a slippery slope, which she had reason to fear could send her sliding back into serious trouble, the kind that she cautiously, somewhat sceptically hoped analysis might help her to transcend. With a history of extreme debt that went along with poly-drug abuse, her view, based on agonizing experience, was that to owe me money would be akin to using cocaine. She had been over her head in debt and variously addicted, and knew all too well the seductively compelling sirens that had repeatedly lured her to self-destruction. To allow her to owe me money would also implicate me in a co-dependent relationship with her,

which would threaten to bring us both to our knees. She told me that, in Debtors Anonymous meetings that she attended, therapist-addicts regularly spoke about how their patients owed them thousands of dollars, enacting collusive co-dependent relationships in which the therapists themselves would incur great debt while waiting impotently, pathetically, for their patients' ever-elusive, tantalizing payment. For these therapists, each session was a roll of the dice, a chance to hope once again that their ship was about to come in and finally get them out of the debt, both literal and symbolic of the morass in which they lived with their patient, that they had themselves incurred. Professional therapists who couldn't collect fees from their patients would sit together with patients who owed their therapists money at these meetings, telling their stories, helping each other with the shared problem which they had often found themselves helpless to conquer in their own personal therapy. (Bass, 2007)

Therapists can feel guilt about allowing patient debt and this makes resolution more difficult for both.

Reparation

The concept of debt is important in practical and conscious terms in most people's lives but it is also apparent through analysis of the unconscious processes. Repaying debt is a theme in analytic work. Eliot shows in Silas Marner that when the Squire's son decides that he must make amends for his silence and deceit by acknowledging Eppie as his daughter, removing her from Marner's cottage so that she can be a lady, she refuses absolutely to leave the man who has brought her up. Godfrey realises, that there are debts we cannot pay in the way that we can repay financial debts. He must live with his debt and forgo the satisfaction of feeling that it has been repaid.

Why do we wish to repair?

Since dealings with money echo the need to trust and to pay debts, the superego (which regulates what we ought to do) is crucial. Fairbairn differed from Freud in the way he conceived the working of the superego. Freud moved towards a position in which the superego is part of the psychical structure but is not conscious. The part of the mind that tells us what we should or should not do is formed through experiences of infancy and childhood, through the influence of parents and others and it causes anxiety when the individual is tending to satisfy instinctual urges and wishes. This concept is important in any consideration of a relation to money and making or spending it. Fairbairn followed Freud in naming the superego as the agency that intervenes in the oedipal triangle of mother, father, and child to prevent the child from seeking gratification through a sexual relationship with a parent. It operates through fear of castration and its primary emotion is guilt. Fairbairn (1946) named a slightly different agency the internal saboteur and regarded its function as being to attack the ego when it was seeking any form of gratification. Since few people now use the term superego in its strictly Freudian sense there is perhaps no need for this distinction but clinical practice certainly shows that guilt and anxiety accompany the use and misuse of money for most people.

Money and guilt

Alice has at least the usual anxiety about her own meanness. She does not want to offer to pay Margaret more than she must but she feels guilty for not offering a very generous fee. Margaret is delaying the opportunity to discover the nature of this guilt by leaving Alice to her own devices in setting the fee. This delay means that Alice has to suffer guilt and begin to think about what it means. Margaret will have to hope that this guilt will manifest itself later or in other ways and will be amenable to analysis. This may well emerge in further accounts of growing up in the mining town which hints at limitations on spending being imposed on the child. Such limitations can lead to guilt because the child is aware that she can damage her parents by spending money that is not easily available.

Guilt for possessing and withholding money is embedded in the rituals that we find in rites of passage throughout the world. Bronislaw Malinowski, the ethnologist, described in his text *Argonauts of the Western Pacific* of 1922 how south sea islanders seek to avoid debt by what appears to be generosity:

> As a result, every time a Kwakiutl gets what he really wants-a wife, a big catch of fish, a new house he feels guilty. He solves

this problem by holding a gift-giving potlatch ritual, where he dumps his guilt and his bad feelings into some blanket-money or copper-money and gives this guilt-money away with his bad feelings inside it. By sharing the guilt-money with his neighbour or by destroying it—throwing it into the fire or into the river—he feels much better. He can then enjoy his wife, fish or home without fear of his extremely punitive superego, without fear of upsetting his parents' severe strictures against pleasure. (1922, p. 87)

Can paying for psychoanalysis sometimes be a form of guilt money? Bruce Fink in a Freud Museum conference of 2010 took as his subject "why would anyone in their right mind want to pay for psychoanalysis?" This is a provocative topic in its own right but it is very germane to the question of the debt and its own relationship to castration. John Forrester concludes that we try to pay off our debts by our actions and by our wishes but that perhaps we are still all seeking something for nothing. In his terms, we are seeking the infantile contentment that we once had before the awareness struck that we have to pay for our pleasures. Paying for our pleasures is one of the main themes of psychoanalysis. People seek therapy because of their debts, not usually financial debts although they may be expressed in financial terms and the guilt that debts induce. Our task is to help the patient track the nature of the guilt further back towards its source and to find a way to live with whatever this means.

CHAPTER TWELVE

Money matters in the consulting room

E very therapist has to deal with his or her own human greed and defences against it. The therapist is also seeking the narcissistic satisfaction of being a therapist as well as having the associated income. Being a therapist requires patients and with them the assurance of having the money from the fees that confirm this status. Greed may take the form of demanding high fees or may be shown in working free of charge or for very low fees. Whatever the financial arrangement, people will challenge it and the therapist will have to deal with all sorts of practical and emotional questions. This chapter will examine the processes that occur in the consulting room where the psyche of the therapist interacts with the psyche of the patient in relation to payment, thefts, debts, and gifts. It will draw on experience in private practice and in a large clinic as well as in the NHS.

Therapist debts

The therapist has her own personal experience of managing money and has managed her training costs. Trainees pay fees for their training, for personal therapy and for supervision. Not all these elements are paid for separately in all institutions. For example, some of the training supervision is included in the fee for those who are training where there is a clinic in which they work. Whatever the payment arrangements each trainee is likely to be very involved with questions of how to pay and what the payment means. Since fees for training as a psychoanalytic psychotherapist can amount to at least £50,000 in London in the early twenty-first century, many people will have to take out loans and will also consider working at another job part or full time in order to fund the training. The way the training body deals with fees is bound to be significant, because it fills a parental role, in providing the experience and learning and therefore the background for future practice of each candidate in training. Even more important will be the model provided by personal therapists and supervisors.

Therapists arrive at their graduation with a considerable debt or at least having spent much of their savings on their training. They will then have to find a way of making a living as a new and inexperienced therapist. This may lead to continuing with another job and fitting any therapeutic work that they find round a full-time job elsewhere. At its worst it leads to a hunger for clinical sessions which can express itself in difficulty in arranging or accepting endings with clients.

Therapist pathology

The sociologist, Paul Halmos, wrote an influential study of the counselling profession as it was in 1965, in which he examined the motivation that leads people to take up what was then a new profession. Good reasons for doing psychological therapy of any kind remain those that have prevailed from the beginning: to earn money and to learn. Undue zeal to help or to change others might be more a matter of dangerous pathology than a suitable motive for setting out to do this work. No-one owns psychoanalysis and as Haya Oakley pointed out, she uses the title psychoanalyst not to claim any form of ownership of psychoanalysis but to say that psychoanalysis owns her (2001, p. 36). She is a member of a psychoanalytic community all of whom accept Freud's two criteria that we work with transference and resistance (Freud, 1913).

Maroda (1991) assesses the therapist's motivation in terms of the wish to learn from the patient and be healed by participating in the process. This would imply a greater equality with the patient than many therapists would think helpful but it supports her polemic that we should be more open about our counter transference responses. Whatever the individual's own personal experience of life and relationships might be, it will affect her ability to understand her patients so that she can endure and work with whatever they bring. Similarly the therapist's own experience of the symbolic emotional framework that structures her attitude to money will make a difference to what she can tolerate and what she can make therapeutic. Like her patients the therapist will have attitudes to money which show that it symbolises the fulfilment of perhaps her possessiveness or her narcissistic needs or her wish to convince herself that she is independent and has her own resources.

Payment

At the beginning of each piece of analytic work the therapist makes an agreement with the patient about whether they will continue to meet after the first session. The therapist has many reasons to wish for payment, not least that it carries her through periods of difficulty when her honest reaction would be to wish to end the therapy. A fee must therefore be set. In Freud's advice on technique, he is clear on the therapeutic necessity for payment and for it to be substantial:

> Gratuitous treatment enormously increases many neurotic resistances such as the temptations of the transference relationship for young women or the opposition to the obligatory gratitude in young men arising from the father complex which is one of the most troublesome obstacles to the treatment ... and the patient is deprived of a useful incentive to exert himself to bring the treatment to an end. (1913)

Both of these points made by Freud are of continuing relevance to both sexes in the consulting room. Women and men could use free therapy to convince themselves that they are loved by the therapist who wants to see them without any reward beyond their presence. A man may feel that free therapy increases his need to be grateful to his father and may either bind him by gratitude or increase his desire to be rid of him. Both of these responses make the process of therapy difficult and may bring it to an untimely end. Akhtar (2009) finds that Jacobs (1986) provided the most lucid statement among recent writers on the need for negotiation of fees at the outset of therapy. Jacobs recommends that contingency plans for hard times should also be discussed. This latter is rarely addressed by therapists at the time of writing although financial stringency might make this more usual. Payment is desirable both for the therapist and for the patient.

Although there are no clear rules about what else should be agreed at the outset, there is now some writing on this subject. In my own book (Murdin, 2005), I attempted to show how the early sessions of an analytic relationship might, as Freud suggested, set a direction for the transference and would in any case determine the likelihood of success for the enterprise. At the very least the patient needs to be told clearly what he must pay and when and how he must pay it. Alice demonstrates some of the difficulty for the patient of not knowing what is expected. For the majority of therapists in the UK in the early twenty-first century, payment means a fee of between £35 and £250 per session (B. Kahr quoted by Brandreth, 2002). Most therapists will also review their fees annually and people must be told that this will happen. Formal complaints have been made by patients who thought that the fee they were given at the beginning would remain the same for the whole of their therapy.

Margaret, the therapist in the case study, gives a great deal of freedom to her patients and sees their pathology in their use of it. Unlike Margaret, most therapists will establish a regular time when the fees must be paid. This is important because it establishes parameters so that departures from them can then be interpreted. Alice suffers from the lack of this but has to work things out for herself.

Therapists in private practice follow their own inclinations over this but a decision needs to be made and followed. Women have been shown to set lower fees on average than men although few would offer such an open policy as Margaret offers to Alice. Mary Burnside relates this tendency to the practice of paying women less than men in other professions (1986, p. 49). The therapist might wish to pause and consider whether she has observed anything of her own pathology in her wish to be paid more or less quickly and whether she will wait for the patient to be ready to pay. For example, the therapist who is very lax over payment and leaves the patient to offer to pay as Margaret does may be demonstrating her own wish to be the all loving mother who has no ordinary greed for money. This may be helpful to some clients but may for some people reactivate the parent who would not set boundaries and who left the rules unclear. Alice is aware that she feels guilty as she did as a child and will need to consider what this means for her in the future.

One common arrangement is that the therapist presents the patient with a written invoice at the end of every month. This invoice will then be paid in the following session, although some people will choose to pay it immediately. For some patients, the monthly system does not work well. These will be principally people on low incomes or with sizeable debts who need to manage their finances very carefully. These people will usually manage better if they pay for each session at the time. In private practice there will perhaps not be many people in this category but most therapists will see one or two people who need help at least initially to meet the demands of regular payment.

Many people feel uncomfortable negotiating the level of the fee. Some therapists, particularly those who are not analytically trained might consider the Freudian theory of the faecal meaning of money to be old fashioned and irrelevant but the distaste for handling money remains and is often greater than any distaste for talking about sexuality or sex. Possibly this is one reason for the setting of a fixed fee with no negotiation. Simply saying "my fee is £50" leaves people the option of finding the money or not taking up the option of therapy. On the other hand, it means that if there is any negotiation over the fee it will be accompanied by the guilt of the patient who cannot or does not choose to pay what he thinks his therapist wants. Others who have trained in an institution that runs a clinic which is seeing people with low incomes may find that they are not always happy to do this and will negotiate if the prospective patient cannot afford the standard fee. In his paper of 1913 Freud made various technical recommendations to physicians who were embarking on psychoanalysis and he points out:

> It is well known that the value of a treatment is not enhanced in a patient's eyes if a very low fee is asked. (1913, p. 176)

And for those who complain of the expense of analysis he points out that:

> Nothing in life is so expensive as illness and foolishness. (1913, p. 178)

The therapist tries to avoid pretensions to generosity and moderates her genuine greed; Some therapists will attempt to relate to the income of the patient but this is not easy to do as "income" is a broad term. There may be a partner who earns very well even though the prospective patient has only a part time job or is incapacitated by anxiety and depression and is not working at all. Given that this can be clarified with the patient, this seems a fair approach to setting a fee. Once income has been established the therapist needs a specific policy that can be applied objectively. For example, charging a certain number of pounds per thousand of income would be a possibility which prevents the therapist from reacting too much on the basis of her own immediate response of liking or disliking or alternatively, feeling sorry for the patient. A hasty decision might lead to resentment later, which will not help anyone unless it can be analysed.

The therapist responding to the counter transference that she experiences like Symington (1986) may underestimate what the patient is capable of achieving. Symington was able to make use of his counter transference reaction when he observed it and thought about it. He was then able to value his patient enough to make an appropriate demand. This shows again how important attitudes to money can be in the overall pathology of the patient.

In addition to making her living, the therapist needs the payment to make her into the therapist that she wants to be. If the patient withholds payment, he is withholding his agreement that she is a therapist at all, much less a good enough therapist. The opposite pressure applies if the therapist sees herself as a philanthropist who enjoys having patients who do not pay her at all but can benefit from her generosity. Her reward might be gratitude which can be exacted like money. A less conscious motivation for low charges may be that the therapist can then feel that it matters less if she is not providing the best possible therapy. Doubts about this are appropriate and necessary but should be discussed in supervision not acted out.

Stealing from the therapist

According to Melanie Klein, the infant suffers from fear that he has emptied his mother's breast and left her impoverished (1959, p. 308). Mothers can react by reinforcing this fear or can help to diminish it by showing that they are in fact surviving. The therapist survives attacks and is available again for the next session. Those who have not resolved their anxiety may feel the need to take and take in order to test whether she does survive. To the therapist, the patient who does not pay what he owes may seem like a thief. He has enjoyed the hospitality of the therapist in her consulting room and has taken advantage of her thinking and her response Therapists feel deprived in this situation. They may also feel duped. This leads to anger which is more dangerous if it is hidden beneath apparent good humour and benevolence. Of course the therapist is in a good position to reflect on her emotions and discuss her reactions in supervision. This will usually prevent acting out of the aggression and will mean that useful and constructive comments can be made about the meaning of the behaviour to the patient. Not all therapists have supervision and not all therapists will discuss their own response in an honest and open way. If they do not, they may become victims, not free agents.

Alice's experience shows what happens to her and those round her when she has to face the loss of a large sum of money through what appears to be a theft. Her reaction shows the way in which theft attacks the normal healthy narcissism that enables us to have self-respect. Even though the theft that she has to face is not of her own personal money, the loss takes away her self-respect and her confidence to the extent that she cannot think clearly. The people round her react in different ways. The Finance Manager sticks to the figures and does not care or notice what he is doing to others when he announces the amount. Julie who is young and confident in her own judgment is adamant about her paranoid fears. The effect on her is that she wants to catch the thief and so defeat the forces that are attacking her and the organisation.

One of the dangers of the effect of a theft is that all anger, hatred, and hostility may be directed at the source of the theft. Alice has the problem that she likes and respects Jacob so her dislike of the trustees grows instead. Not being able to feel straightforward hatred and anger leaves her confused and weakened. Therapists who feel deceived by a patient are in something of the same position. Freud wrote of the effect of losing a loved person as being like losing a part of one's thinking self (1917). Only time and the gradual acceptance of the loss will enable the bereaved person to take back possession of his own self.

Payment as relief of tension

Alice is unsure about whether she is faced with a theft or a debt when Jacob seems to be accused of taking money from her charity. In either case, something has been taken from her. She has settled her own financial debt to her therapist with some pain. In her case the payment is important not so much because it represents a sacrifice as because it represents something that she wishes to give to her therapist and so the fee means a great deal to her. She is relieved when she has paid although the process gives her an experience of anger with her therapist which is difficult for her to process on her own.

Up to the present day in the early twenty-first century, most analytic therapists have expected or required their patients to pay them by cheque. Perhaps this is an element of the predominantly middle-class status of those who provide and go to therapy. Cheques have meant that there is a moment at which the debt is cancelled out at least in monetary terms. Payment by cheque means that there is a person to person transaction and it is immediately apparent whether the debt has been paid in full or not. The future of this method of payment is now in some doubt. Patients are asking to pay by Bank Transfer which will be done online so that the money passes from one account to another and the therapist will have to pay attention to know whether the debt has been paid or not and will find out in communion with her computer, not with the patient. The only thing that passes between the two will be the invoice which is given to the patient. The debt is always in the patient's court and this could be useful if it is considered material for interpretation.

Debt is an important concept in the therapeutic lexicon. The infant owes everything to his mother or primary carer as he could not survive alone. All human beings begin with this position of helplessness and spend the rest of their lives achieving more or less independence and with a greater or lesser degree of anxiety. The therapeutic situation inevitably has some echoes of this since at the beginning the therapist is likely to be the only one who has any idea of how the therapy might progress or at least knows that she does not know. Many patients hope, quite reasonably that the therapy will bring answers to the questions that they are posing consciously or unconsciously. This puts the therapist in the position of the one who is supposed to know. She holds the rights to all the debts that the patient owes until she is able to specify what they are and disentangle them.

The fee as money

Whatever the meaning to the patient, the therapist must be paid her fee. Parameters need to be set for the method of payment. Part of the urge to rid oneself of all debt may lead to a wish to see the debt being cancelled immediately. Questions may then arise over whether therapists will allow patients to pay in cash or to pay in advance. Arguments can be made that being paid in cash puts the therapist on the level of the tradesman who may give a discount for cash to avoid paying tax. Cash gives rise to a possible association also with the profession of prostitution because as Halmos (1965) pointed out, the therapist may be offering a form of love or at least concern and benevolent interest. He refers to Sandor Ferenczi who said that "the psychoanalytic cure is in direct proportion to the cherishing love given by the psychoanalyst to the patient." Ferenczi experimented with much more active techniques than Freud and even in some cases where an impasse had been reached, he offered the patient the opportunity to analyse him so that the process was mutual and the debt was incurred equally by both. He stopped this practice partly because of the difficulty of speaking freely without compromising the confidentiality of his other patients (1920). Nevertheless, casework among social workers in the 1960s in the UK was still following some of the principles of mutuality and shared responsibility. Halmos (1965) cites M. L. Sheppard who wrote of offering:

> ten years of unsparing friendship between caseworker and client, floral tributes brought along personally to the funeral of client's husband, taking client out to lunches, gifts and presents, and every sign of warm and sustained mutuality. (1965, p. 52)

This kind of cure by love was implied by the attempts to repair deficits of love in Ferenczi's practice (1920). He believed that the active agent in therapeutic work was the therapeutic gift of love: tolerating severe regressions and emphasising the holding, containing, corrective parental function of the analyst. Ferenczi witnessed and described primitive defence mechanisms in the service of psychic survival. These included dissociative states, identification with the aggressor, splitting, and fragmentation. The difficulties and dangers of offering love without limit were, however, recognised as a result of his therapeutic experiments.

Following what was learned from Ferenczi's work, Elizabeth Irvine, a psychoanalytic social worker wrote of the work of the social worker, Octavia Hill, who offered emotional warmth to her very deprived cases (1956):

> Such relationships ... were not however easy to maintain; the early literature of social work contains much evidence of the struggle

> to walk this way between the Scylla of over-indulgence (based
> on guilt towards the deprived and outcast) and the Charybdis of
> self-righteous contempt for the "undeserving" (based on paranoid
> anxieties about the danger of insatiable exploitation by these dam-
> aged clients). (1956, p. 54)

The overall effect of these attempts to offer explicit and tangible tokens
of the therapist's love has been an uneasy recognition that when we ask
for payment, we are asking for payment for a form of love, or at least
for positive regard.

Why must people pay for this form of love?

Why not work free of charge? Freud' was not offering love, only
analysis and his views on payment were clear. See p. 155. There are
other reasons. Since psychotherapy, psychoanalysis, and counselling
are all now regarded as professions and have lengthy and expensive
training for practitioners to undergo before they can register with
the reputable umbrella organisations that exist in most countries
now, the therapists need to earn a living and in many cases pay off
debts incurred in training. Unless the fees are paid by insurance or
another agency, the patients will have to enable this work to be done
by paying for it.

Therapists defend their charging policies in a variety of ways. A major
theme in this defence has been that paying fees helps the patient.
Lorand and Console (1958) investigated the hypothesis, following Freud
(1913), that free therapy increases resistance. They carried out research
on fifty-nine analysands in a free clinic and found that the difficulties
in treating this group "were very little different from the general difficulties which are found in the office [private] practice." (1958, p. 63).
Arguments in favour of free treatment have mostly followed Freud in
saying that the patient would be bound by gratitude and would not
be able to feel or express negative transference. Self-respect is another
argument that has been cited in favour of the patient making a contribution. While working in a free clinic in the National Health Service,
I frequently encountered patients who felt that they should not take up
my time "there must be many people who are worse off than me." This
provided material for analytic work of course, but the drop-out rate
was higher for such people.

There is still a strong tradition of generosity which may have a
pathological origin in the therapist. Halmos (1965) emphasised that

the new counselling profession shared "the assumptions and values of the new philanthropic expertise of helping through caring-listening-prompting." He adds that these new professionals betray a "tender mindedness" of which they seem ashamed and that counselling had its origins in the desire to do good. What Halmos does not mention is that many of those practising counselling were paid practitioners of an existing profession such as medicine or psychiatric social work and therefore had their own income from other sources (1965, p. 2). Freud says that he carried out an experiment, offering one free hour in order to see whether any desirable results appeared. He found that resistances increased. (1913, p. 177).

Of course, the argument for the payment of fees is not simply a matter of the therapist earning a living. Freud was clear that the psychoanalyst should charge high fees in order that the patient would take the work very seriously and would work hard to reach the end. Certainly, looking forward to the ending of the payment of fees is a factor which can help people to end their otherwise interminable attachment to the therapy and therapist although it is not clear that it always helps the therapy itself to move faster.

Therapist competence

Therapists have their own unconscious processes in relation to charging and not charging. Many newly qualified therapists have some level of diffidence about their competence and may be tempted to charge low fees because this will make them feel less anxious about what they can deliver. The truth is that no analytic therapist can be sure of any given outcome and many would deny that specific outcomes are sought. Analytic therapy is essentially an open-ended enterprise in which two people set out to discover what they can about their mental processes in order to make more of the unconscious available to the conscious mind. This will be done to a greater or lesser extent but is not often the conscious purpose of the patient and many therapists worry about what they are offering and what they can deliver. Nevertheless, this does not constitute a reason for not charging. No hairdresser would consider not charging clients because the final effect might not fulfil their dreams. Only if demonstrable harm has been done equivalent to damage to the scalp, is there a reason for guilt to lead to financial reparation.

Charging fees and being paid reassures the therapist that she is doing something worthwhile even when she is not sure exactly what good she is achieving. Nevertheless, her identity may depend on her work and as McLaughlin points out:

> The intensity of the therapist's sense of identity as the good physician vitally determines how he chooses his patients, where he sets his limits, and even his definition of what is included in "classical analytic technique." In any community of analysts it quickly becomes known to all that some are "wearers of the hair shirt" and will undertake difficult and demanding cases, and that others are oppositely self-protective in their case selection and technical approach. But the most striking instances of this identity issue, almost in caricatured degree, are to be found among analysts-in-training who are themselves children of physicians or derived from a background in which the figure of the doctor had especially powerful significance. Here there is often an especial poignancy to the Aesculapian[1] dynamics, and the freedom to act with enlightened self-interest can be so curtailed as to approach masochism. Their identity encumberment is particularly evident in their dealing with the patient's hostility as expressed in fee manipulations and self-destructiveness, both issues which impinge sharply upon the stereotype of the physician. These therapists tend to come off badly in any battle of the fee, hardly can stomach Freud's dictum of hire by the hour, and endure many inroads upon time, patience, and income. They tend to be easily driven into some activity parameter when their motives are questioned or their therapeutic potency threatened by the patient's becoming sicker or threatening a self-destructive act. Their shame and hostility mount with the continued therapeutic stalemate or the rising unpaid bill, and the defences utilized by them against these affects are shaped in part by the commitment to the "kindly doctor" ideal. (1961, pp. 117–118)

Marketing and loss leaders

Although most on-going therapy in the UK is paid for directly by the patient practice is more variable in the assessment session. There seems to be a commercial interest as well as perhaps a charitable desire to offer an opportunity for people with no experience of therapy to discover whether it might be of use to them. So, for example, a group of therapists (Clinic for Lacanian Psychoanalysis, 2011) made the following statement on their website:

> The initial consultation is free of charge. Our main aim is to be open and available to anyone who wants to speak to an analyst about the problems they have encountered. Fees for follow up sessions will be negotiable and agreeing them will take into account ability to pay. This can be discussed with your analyst at the time of the first meeting where your personal circumstances are taken into consideration.

Individual therapists working separately have variable practice and do have some negative feelings if there is competition for work and they see some colleagues making "free introductory offers" which may seem unfair or inappropriate and unprofessional. Again each therapist must make up her own mind about how she charges for the assessment but she could consider how a free session will seem to the patient. The site quoted above makes it clear that this is a one-off concession but the rationale is not so clear. Presumably the therapists wish to give potential patients a taste of what therapy might be like and so give them a motivation for finding the financial means to access it.

Charging for missed sessions

The assessment session is the point at which the therapist also needs to tackle the question of payment for missed sessions. Freud's advice is clear: the patient leases an hour of the therapist's time on a regular basis and must pay for it whether or not he is actually there to use it. If you rent a garage, you will not be excused from the rent because you did not use it one night. Those who make a living from private practice cannot afford to allow patients to stay away whenever they have some problem with attendance. That is a good enough reason to charge when the contract is broken by the patient, but it is not the most important reason. As Freud pointed out, the missed session is often a resistance and the therapist must do her job and figure out what happened in the previous sessions that could have led to a need to absent oneself from the risks of the next session. This is always a useful consideration but is essential when the reason given is dubious in some way or is simply the casual

"I forgot." Patients are often very resistant to this kind of consideration and therapists frequently make excuses to themselves for not enforcing their own policy. The excuse-making process is most likely to appear when the patient has a very good reason for non-attendance such as illness or lack of transport. The question at its root though is clear: who should pay for this problem, the patient or the therapist? Those with independent means who are not wholly dependent on this income may be willing to say that they will bear the loss themselves. This is partly at least from care for the vulnerable and suffering patient but it is also an avoidance of the anger of the patient who has a range of emotional reasons for hating being charged for these sessions.

Therapists may tie themselves in knots over charging since they usually charge in arrears. Difficulties arise when a patient leaves and there is some dispute over the question of whether the patient was expected for the session or not:

> Dr P had been seeing a therapist J for six years and had benefitted from the therapy but in the last month she had felt that it was no longer as useful as it had been. The effort of getting to the early morning sessions had become onerous and she thought that she was ready to stop. She told her therapist that she would like to end and the therapist simply said "I think you are avoiding moving on to the next important issue that you need to face." Dr P could not think of any important issues and told him so. He merely shrugged and said no more. She thought that maybe she would understand in a few weeks. Nothing came to her and she still wished to finish. The next time she sent an e mail saying that she wished to end and would not attend any more sessions. J responded with an e mail saying that such a sudden ending was not wise and that he would hope to see her at her next session to discuss "her problem." If she did not wish to attend she was to let him know. She did not respond and the next thing she knew was that she received an invoice for the session she had not attended. She was very upset about this and after a few weeks she submitted a formal complaint. J believed that he was acting in Dr P's interests in "giving her firm boundaries."

This account may have resonances for many of us. Mediation was able to bring about a better ending and it seemed clear that J was doing what he genuinely thought was best but he now thinks that he will work harder on endings when they are raised by the patient and he acknowledges that money in the shape of his income was one of the strands that made him so reluctant to allow an ending.

Refusing to give

For the patient, a missed session is always an attack. Matte-Blanco showed that in the dynamic unconscious postulated by Freud, there is a process which Matte-Blanco named bilogic. In this system of the unconscious, there is logical symmetry. "I have left you" = "You have left me." (1988, p. 81) The patient may unconsciously resent the therapist for not being there for the session when in agreed reality it was he who was not there. Some people will be able to recognise that they indeed do feel this although others will think the therapist is mad or defensive for saying so. Even without the deeply unconscious operation of bilogic, the patient is likely to feel deprived and being asked to pay is adding insult to injury. The mother who absented herself from a hungry baby is now asking the baby to pay for his deprivation.

Some therapists have developed a policy that if they are given at least twenty four hours' notice of a missed session, they will not charge. The logic of this is difficult to see, as hardly any therapist can suddenly arbitrarily make use of a vacant slot within twenty-four hours. The only thing to be said for it is that the therapist can go home or stay at home and need not wait in the consulting room. On the whole it seems a less professional way of working and probably relates to the more charitable origins of counselling in the work of pastoral therapists and the followers of Carl Rogers in the United States.

Problems with enforcing payment for missed sessions may occur at any time in a therapy but they are particularly difficult and dangerous at the time when a patient is ambivalent about continuing therapy:

> A therapist, Sarah was seeing a patient, Michael. He was a young man of 27 who came with difficulties with his partner who wanted a baby when he did not feel ready to get married, much less have a baby. He said several times in his assessment session "I'm not saying never, I'm just not ready yet." He was also having problems with his boss and had driven his company car into his boss's car in the company car park. He thought the car was parked "like he was asking for trouble" but was in his third session beginning to

acknowledge that perhaps the boss was standing in for his father who had been dominating and physically abusive, hitting Michael's mother and shouting abuse at all his four children. He failed to attend for the next session and left no message. Sarah was anxious because she thought he might have decided that "just not yet" was how he felt about his therapy. She wrote him a note after he missed the next session and had still not communicated. She then received a text message saying that he had been held up at work but would come next week. At this point she revealed to her supervisor that he was paying in cash for each session at the end of the session. She did not want to charge him for the two missed sessions because she thought it would be hard enough to hold him without "deliberately" making him angry in this way. Her supervisor asked her how she thought that the assumption that he should pay for the two previous sessions as well as the current one would relate to his transference position. After some thought she considered that if she asked for the money she would constellate that dominating father who assumed that he had a right to everything and everyone in the family and if she failed to carry out her own policy she ran the risk of behaving like the mother who had been beaten by the father. This she could interpret of course, but it carried with it the implication that Michael had become the bullying father and that he might have to say "not yet" in order to avoid taking on this role. Having clarified this in her own mind she was able to say to him that, as he already knew, it was her policy to charge for all sessions but that he might have some strong feelings about being asked to pay for the two sessions which presumably his boss had demanded of him. He agreed that he found it difficult to be between his boss and his therapist, but he was glad that his therapist was not giving in like his mother. "I suppose I have no choice but to take this on and still be a man in my own right no matter what is going on around me." This was a remarkable statement and Sarah was both surprised and pleased. He said also that he thought it was very unfair to make him pay for something that he had not had but perhaps he did have a choice after all.

This case was resolved to the extent that the patient continued to attend for the time being and did pay, under protest, for his missed sessions. There have been more difficult situations in which the therapists have been less measured and thoughtful than Sarah. One example led to a complaint. A patient wrote to her therapist to say that she did not wish to attend therapy any more. The therapist wrote back saying that she thought they ought to meet at least once more to end the therapy more appropriately as it had gone on for almost two years,. She offered a date and time and asked the patient to let her know if she was not going to attend. The patient did not attend and did not communicate any further. The therapist then sent her a bill for the previous month's sessions and included the session that was offered but not taken up. The patient paid the invoice but was furious and made a formal complaint for several reasons, including the charging for the "missed session." This aspect of the complaint was upheld and one of the consequences was that the therapist was required to refund the fee for the missed session. There seems little doubt that no therapist should charge for sessions that the patient never agreed to attend even though the therapist offered them in good faith and for good reasons.

Giving something extra

Patients may sometimes be reluctant to pay for sessions that they have not been given but they may, on the other hand, have many different reasons for wishing to give more to their therapists. This often happens at Christmas or one of the times of year that has significance for their culture. Final leaving is another time when gifts are likely to appear. The word "appear" is used advisedly as some patients choose to leave a present behind when they go so that the therapist would find it difficult to return it or not accept it or even interpret the giving. This is very tempting for the therapist and it seems likely that the great majority of therapists will have accepted some if not all of the presents that have been offered to them. These mostly take the form of flowers or a bottle of wine or spirits or of something edible like chocolates. If these are consumed, they are soon gone and the therapist might not feel guilty for long. But why should she feel guilty at all?

The answer to this last question is that the gift, even of this relatively small kind does have meaning and should usually be interpreted rather than consumed. But why should it not be both interpreted and consumed? The arguments go something like: The patient is trying to find an additional way of making himself loved by the therapist and should manage with the same fee as everyone else. The patient is trying to make up for being so full of hate and anger that the therapist cannot put up with him. If the therapist accepts the gift and then interprets, the force of the interpretation may be lost. Interpreting first and then accepting the gift seems on the other hand to undermine the validity of the interpretation. So, for example, saying to a patient who brings a bottle of wine before the Christmas holiday, "You would like to be involved in my celebrations and if you imagine me drinking this, you might be able to imagine drinking it with me" might or might not be a correct or useful interpretation of the patient's unconscious or dimly perceived motive, but if the therapist then says "Thank you" and takes the wine he might make it seem that he is prepared to act out the desired scenario. Alternatively, he might say that he will accept the wine and will subtract something from the fee that the patient is due to pay. A more rigorous analytic therapist might say, "I would like you to take it with you. Your fee is enough to give me." This implies another line of interpretation which is the patient's wish to do more than he is required to do. He might wish to be a favoured patient or he might feel that he has to make up for his appalling material with extra gifts, in other words a kind of bribe to persuade the therapist to put up with him.

Of course there are other reasons for gifts, especially those given at the end of therapy and one of those might be gratitude. The patient may wish to express his gratitude, having dealt with his paranoid schizoid ambivalence. The therapist might seem to be rejecting the change if she does not accept the gift. The only way of deciding whether this is the case is to judge each occasion separately and on its own merits. Needless to say, accepting large gifts or gifts of money is unethical and should never be done regardless of the patient's motivation as the therapist who does so lays herself open to accusations of exploiting vulnerability.

Unresolved debt

The last area to consider in relation to the payment of fees in the consulting room is debt that cannot be resolved because it remains after the patient has left. If the patient is allowed to build up a debt of unpaid fees that is not dealt with by interpretation the therapist may be faced with a decision about the collection of debts after the ending. Not many therapists would pursue a patient with anything other than a personal letter asking for the payment to be made. In fact in an informal survey

I have not come across any therapist who has used the Small Claims Court which is available for redress in the UK.

Small claims court offers a legal process which can lead to a visit by bailiffs threatening to seize goods to pay the debt. In order to begin the process there would need to be a series of letters warning of the intention to involve debt collectors. The difficulty here is that patients who leave without paying are probably either indigent or angry and most therapists would consider that such a situation is something that she should have been able to avoid if she had done her job well enough. For this narcissistic reason she might hesitate to enforce payment. She will probably be angry with the patient and will often recognise that this is a sign that her own work on herself was not complete. Bringing in an outside agency would also be a betrayal of confidentiality and even if she is willing to do this for the one patient who owes her a large amount, she needs to consider the general wellbeing of the profession and the importance of the principle of never betraying the identity of patients. Finally, she might recognise that her patient cannot afford to pay her and that his need is greater than hers and she will just have to write off the debt. In all and for whatever combination of reasons, the therapist is unlikely to make a public display of her patient and her own failure to help him to manage his debt.

The vast majority of clinicians work with humanity and intelligence in order to make the process useful to their patients. The task is to balance the needs of the therapist to earn a living against the difficulties of the financial vicissitudes of her patients. She can try not to be so draconian that they disappear underground and to manage the money so that the patient is safely and firmly held within a therapeutic frame.

Note

1. Aesculpalian: related to the healing arts.

CONCLUSION

Wishing for money is not infantile. The infant may wish for power, for control for erotic satisfaction, for love but he does not wish for money. The adult with all his complexity begins to understand that money symbolises much of what he wants or he thinks he wants. The analytic therapist helps people, to discover what they really want. Because money symbolises the heart's desire and is bound up with the therapeutic process itself, each analytic therapist needs to analyse her own relationship to money and to its symbolic power. The process gives her a unique opportunity to help people to establish their own values and to discover what money can actually achieve and what it cannot. To say that money does not bring happiness is a cliché with some truth. Money can bring education, health, and understanding. On the other hand, it does this only because it can be exchanged for many things although not for our most profound needs for love and concern, for wisdom and intellectual and aesthetic pleasures. The therapeutic enterprise can bring freedom from the prison of the over valuation of money and also freedom to hold a measured and rational view of what money is and can do.

REFERENCES

Abramson, R. (2001). A cost-effective psychoanalytic treatment of a severely disturbed woman. *Journal of American Academy of Psychoanalysis*, 29: 245–264.

Akhtar, S. (2009). *Turning Points in Dynamic Psychotherapy*. London: Karnac.

Arnaud, G. (2003). Money as signifier: A Lacanian insight into the monetary order. *Free Associations*, 10: 35–43.

Bass, A. (2007). When the frame doesn't fit the picture. *Psychoanalytic Dialogues*, 17: 1–27.

Berghout, C. C., Zevalkink, J. & Hakkaart-van Roijen, L. (2010). A cost-utility analysis of psychoanalysis versus psychoanalytic psychotherapy. *International Journal of Technology Assessment in Health Care*, 26: 3–10.

Bion, W. R. (1967). *Second Thoughts*. London: Karnac.

Bollas, C. & Sundelson, D. (1995). *The New Informants*. London: Karnac.

Bowlby, J. (1975). *Attachment and Loss*. Harmondsworth: Penguin Books.

Brandreth, G. (2002). Everything you always wanted to know about Freud but were too afraid to ask. *The Sunday Telegraph*, 12 May. Available at: http://www.fortunecity.com/emachines/e11/86/freud.html [accessed 16 May 2012].

Brenner, R. (1986/2007). The social basis of economic development. In: J. Brenner (Ed.), *Analytical Marxism* (pp. 3–7). Cambridge: Cambridge University Press.

Burnside, M. (1986). Fee practices of male and female therapists. In: D. W. Krueger (Ed.), *The Last Taboo* (pp. 48–55). New York: Brunner Mazell.

Chicago Association for Psychoanalytic Psychology. (2011). Available at: http://www.chicagotherapistfinder.com/about.htm [accessed 16 May 2012].

Clinic for Lacanian Psychoanalysis. (2011). Available at: http://www.lacanianpsychoanalysis.co.uk/fees

Coles, P. (2003). *The Importance of Sibling Relationships in Psychoanalysis.* London: Karnac.

Dickens, C. (1857/2003). *Little Dorrit*. Harmondsworth: Penguin Books.

Dickens, C. (1860/2004). *Great Expectations*. Harmondsworth: Penguin Classics.

Eliot, G. (1861/2008). *Silas Marner*. Oxford: World Classics.

Eliot, G. (1874/2008). *Middlemarch: A Study of Provincial Life*. Oxford: World Classics.

Fairbairn, W. R. D. (1946). Object-relationships and dynamic structure. *International Journal of Psycho-Analysis, 27*: 30–37. Reprinted in: Fairbairn, W. R. D. (1952). *Psychoanalytic Studies of the Personality*. London: Routledge & Kegan, 137–151.

Faulks, S. (2009). *A Week in December*. London: Vintage Books.

Ferenczi, S. (1920/1950). Further development of an active therapy in psychoanalysis. In: J. Suttle (Ed.), *Further Contributions to the Theory and Practice of Psychoanalysis*. London: Maresfield.

Forrester, J. (1997). *Truth, Lies, Money and Psychoanalytic Games*. Cambridge, MA: Harvard University Press.

Freedman, N., Hoffenberg, J. D., Vorus, N. & Frosch, A. (1999). The effectiveness of psychoanalytic psychotherapy: The role of treatment duration, frequency of sessions, and the therapeutic relationship. *Journal of the American Psychoanalytic Association, 47*: 741–772.

Freud, S. (1909a). Analysis of a phobia in a five-year-old boy. *S. E., 10*: 3–149. London: Hogarth Press.

Freud, S. (1909b). Notes upon a case of obsessional neurosis. *S. E., 10*: 152–249. London: Hogarth Press.

Freud, S. (1913). On beginning the treatment. *S.E., 12*: 121–144. London: Hogarth Press.

Freud, S. (1915a). Instincts and their vicissitudes. *S.E., 14*: 917–940. London: Hogarth Press.

Freud, S. (1917). Mourning and melancholia. *S.E.*, *14*: 239–258. London: Hogarth Press.

Freud, S. (1919). Lines of advance in psycho-analytic theory. *S.E.*, *17*: 157–168. London: Hogarth Press.

Freud, S. (1920). Beyond the pleasure principle. *S. E.*, *18*: 1–64. London: Hogarth Press.

Freud, S. (1924). The economic problem of masochism. *S. E.*, *19*: 157–170. London: Hogarth Press.

Freud, S. (1930). Civilisation and its discontents. *S. E.*, *21*: 59–145. London: Hogarth Press.

Fromm, E. (1942/2004). *The Fear of Freedom*. London: Routledge.

Furedi, F. (2003). *Therapy Culture: Cultivating Vulnerability in an Uncertain Age*. London: Routledge.

Furedi, F. (2011). Homepage. Available at: http://www.kent.ac.uk/sspssr/staff/academic/furedi.html [accessed 17 May 2012].

Gedo, J. (1963). A note on non-payment of psychiatric fees. *International Journal of Psychoanalysis*, *44*: 368–371.

Gerard, R. (1991/2000). *A Theatre of Envy*. Leominster: Gracewing.

Grunbaum, A. (1986). *The Foundations of Psychoanalysis*. Berkeley: University of California Press.

Halmos, P. (1965). *The Faith of the Counsellors*. London: Constable.

Hinshelwood, R. (1994). *Clinical Klein*. London: Free Association Books.

Horney, K. (1922/1967). *Feminine Psychology*. New York: Norton.

Howard, K., Kopta, S., Krauss, M. & Orlinsky, D. (1986). The Dose effect in Relationship in Psychotherapy. *American Psychologist*, *41*: 159–164.

Irvine, E. (1956). Transference and reality in the casework relationship. *The British Journal of Psychiatric Social Work*, *III*: 15–24.

Jacobs, D. (1986). On negotiating fees with psychotherapy and psycho-analytic patients. In: D. Krueger (Ed.), *The Last Taboo* (pp. 121–135). New York: Bruner Mazel.

Klein, M. (1959/1984). Our adult world and its roots in infancy. In: *The Writings of Melanie Klein Vol. 3: Envy and Gratitude* (pp. 247–263). London: Hogarth Press.

Lacan, J. (1966a, 1977). A. Sheridan (Trans.). Écrits. Paris: Seuil and London: Routledge.

Lacan, J. (1966b). Le Stade du Miroir comme formateur de la function du Je. In: *Écrits* (pp. 1–7). Paris: Editions Seuil.

Lacan, J. (1973). Television. Paris: Seuil.

Layard, R. (2006). *The Depression Report*. London: The Centre for Economic Performance's Mental Health Policy Group.

Leader, D. (2004). Can there be a monopoly on psychoanalysis? In: A. Casement, (Ed.), *Who Owns Psychoanalysis?* (pp. 245–260). London: Karnac.

Lorand, S. & Console, R. W. (1958). Therapeutic results in psychoanalytic treatment without fee. *International Journal of Psychoanalysis, 39*: 59–65.

McEvoy, T. J. (2001). Private property rights, a look at its history and future. *Fruit Notes, 66*: 40. Reprinted from *Farming, the Journal of Northeast Agriculture, 4*: 45–47.

McLaughlin, James, T. "The analyst and the Hoppocratic Oath" (1961). *Journal of the American Psychoanalytic Association, 9*: 106–123.

McPherson, I. (2011, March). New directions. *New Associations: Journal of the British Psychoanalytic Council*, (5)2.

Malinowski, B. (1922). *Argonauts of the Western Pacific: An Account of Native Enterprise and Adventure in the Archipelagos of Melanesian New Guinea.* London: Routledge & Kegan Paul.

Maroda, K. (1991). *The Power of Counter Transference.* Chichester: John Wiley.

Marx, K. (1844/1959). *Economic and Philosophical Manuscripts.* Moscow: Progress.

Matte-Blanco, I. (1988). *Thinking, Feeling and Being.* London: Routledge.

Mauss, M. (1922/1990). *The Gift: Forms and Functions of Exchange in Archaic Societies.* London: Routledge.

Molino, A. (Ed.) (2001). *Where Id Was.* London: Continuum.

Murdin, L. (2005). *Setting Out.* London: Routledge.

Oakley, H. (2001). What is a psychoanalyst? In A. Molino (Ed.), *Where Id Was* (pp. 222–233). London: Continuum.

Project Nim. (2011). Dir. Martin, J. BBC Films London.

Reiss-Schimmel, I. (1993). *La Psychoanalyse et L'Argent.* Paris: Editions Odile Jacob.

Robertson, J. & Robertson, J. (1969). John, aged 17 Months, for 9 Days in a Residential Nursery. London: Robertson Films.

Roudinesco, E. (2004). The geography of psychoanalysis: Sovereignty, ownership and dispossession. In: A. Casement (Ed.), *Who Owns Psychoanalysis?* London: Karnac.

Rustin, M. (2001). *Reason and Unreason.* London: Continuum.

Sheptun, A. (2011). Philosophy of money. The Paideia Project. Available at: http://www.bu.edu/wcp/Papers/Econ/EconShep.htm [accessed 17 May 2012].

Simmel, G. (1907). *Philosophie des Geldes.* (2nd edn). Leipzig: Duncker and Humblot.

Slap, J. (1976). A note on silent gratifications. *Psychoanalytic Quarterly, 45*: 131–132.

Smith, A. (1750/2004). *Wealth of Nations*. Oxford: World Classics.

Spitz, R. A. (1965). *The First Year of Life: A Psychoanalytic Study of Normal and Deviant Development of Object Relations*. New York: International Universities Press.

Symington, N. (1986). The analyst's act of freedom as an agent of therapeutic change. In: G. Kohon (Ed.), *The British School of Psychoanalysis* (pp. 253–272). London: Free Association Books. Titmuss, R. (1970). *The Gift Relationship*. New York: Pantheon Books.

Tuckett, D. (2011). *Minding the Markets*. London: Palgrave Macmillan.

Winnicott, D. W. (1953). Transitional objects and transitional phenomena—a study of the first not-me possession. *International Journal of Psychoanalysis, 34*: 89–97.

INDEX